AUSTRALIAN
STORIES
For the Soul

D1533075

AUSTRALIAN
STORIES
For the Soul

STRAND PUBLISHING

Sydney

Australian Stories for the Soul
© Copyright 2001 Strand Publishing
Copyright of the individual stories remains the property of the
contributors.

First published 2001 by Strand Publishing

ISBN 187 682 5561

Distributed in Australia by:
Family Reading Publications
B100 Ring Road
Ballarat Victoria 3352
Phone: 03 5334 3244
Fax: 03 5334 3299
Email: enquiries@familyreading.com.au

Unless otherwise noted, all Scripture quotations are taken from the
Holy Bible: New International Version. Copyright © 1973, 1978, 1984 by the
International Bible Society.

Scripture quotations marked KJV are from the *Holy Bible*, King James Version.

This book is copyright. No part of this publication may be reproduced, stored in
a retrieval system, or transmitted in any form or by any means – electronic,
mechanical, photocopy, recording, or any other – except for brief quotations in
printed reviews, without prior permission of the publisher.

Cover photography courtesy of Ken Duncan Australia Wide Pty Ltd,
© Ken Duncan.

Compiled by David and Rachel Dixon
Edited by Owen Salter
Cover design by Joy Lankshear
Typeset by Midland Typesetters, Maryborough, Victoria
Printed by Griffin Press, Netley, South Australia

Contents

v

Granny Smith—A Parable of Australia

Mal Garvin

~⚬~

Maria Ann Smith, who lies buried in St Anne's Anglican Church, Ryde, Sydney, was the midwife for the township of Eastwood. Present at the birth of so many young Australians in that region, she developed a special place in their affections, hence her name 'Granny' Smith.

Maria Smith was a battling Aussie pioneer woman. Her husband's illness meant she had the task, not only of caring for her family and being a midwife, but also of running a small farm and orchard.

On one occasion, after taking a load of her produce to Paddy's Market in Sydney, she chose to buy a small barrel of crab apples to make apple tarts. On bringing them home she found she could use only half the barrel—the rest had unfortunately gone bad.

Deciding to keep the barrel for other uses, she emptied the bad apples on a bit of a garbage pile she had near a creek at

1

the end of the property. Some months later, she returned to discover a small tree pushing its way through the rubbish and noticed by the shape of the leaf that it was an apple tree. She then transplanted the tree and nurtured it. In time it grew strong and produced a batch of green apples, with a previously unknown, but quite appealing, taste. They became particularly popular around Eastwood, where they were affectionately called 'Granny Smith's Apples', and that green Aussie apple has now been accepted throughout the world.

As the children she had helped bring to birth grew up, as fine, lanky, good-natured young currencies, they used to think it was funny that Granny Smith had been responsible for their births but would be remembered most for playing midwife to an apple. 'Isn't that just like God?' she said. 'The very stuff that we chuck away, he uses to bring in a new thing.'

Waiting for Rainbows

Ken Duncan

❧

For over a week, I had been in Colorado searching for that quintessential shot of wildflowers in a mountain setting. My time was running out, as I was due to return to Australia the following day. I had found a beautiful location in Yankee Boy Basin but the morning light had been bland, not allowing the area to fully reveal its beauty. To make matters worse, many other photographers had joined me and were trampling through the fields on their own quests. One particular photographer was so absorbed in his own journey that he would walk right in front of where others had set up to shoot, often flattening the flowers as he went.

I was getting a bit irritated at his selfish attitude and was almost at the point of offering a few pointers on photo etiquette. The guy was like an insect—buzzing around, landing here, landing there—being generally annoying. I knew I shouldn't be angry, but I was, and it was useless to pretend otherwise. I realised that the way I was feeling was wrong and in that frame of mind I would not be sensitive to God's presence nor able to capture the spirit of the moment in this place. So I left that location and went for a drive.

Travelling through the wonderful Colorado countryside, my anger washed away. I marvelled at the awesome creation around me and how small I was in comparison. At peace once more, I asked God where he wanted me to go and felt he wanted me to revisit the site of my earlier frustration.

When I returned to the location, the weather had turned really cloudy and overcast and had chased away all the other photographers. I wondered whether I had misunderstood God. What could I possibly photograph in these conditions? Then I felt God was telling me to set my gear up and get ready to take a shot. I had nothing better to do, so why not?

After I was all set up, it began to rain. There I sat under a huge multi-coloured umbrella looking very obviously like an idiot out in a field getting rained on. Two hours passed with people occasionally driving by. With looks of amazement, they would look my way. I was really bored with the rain and began to ponder the situation. I suggested to God that if he could just give me a small break in the clouds and let the light through, maybe we could have a little rainbow. After all, nothing is impossible with God!

Suddenly there was a huge clap of thunder that made my hair stand on end. I thought either God had heard me and was going to do something or I was going to be hit by lightning. So guess what happened? It rained ever harder! I tried to cover up as best I could and wondered whether I was kidding myself. But I was not ready to give in. I still believed God was going to come through, so I decided not to worry about getting drenched but to stick it out.

The torrential rain only lasted about ten minutes. Then the clouds parted slightly, the sun broke through for a few brief moments and a marvellous rainbow appeared over the field of wild flowers. It was absolutely breathtaking—far more spectacular then I had dared to imagine—and I was there alone to capture the glorious spectacle on film. Just as another photographer arrived and took out his camera, the magnificent light disappeared. The other photographer ran up to me and said, 'Man, you were lucky!' I replied, 'No, I was blessed.'

The moral of the story is—have faith. We often need to stand firm through the rainy season until the blessing comes, as it takes a little rain to bring forth rainbows in our lives.

Walk with Me

Jim Stallard

~

Jim Stallard was deputy director of the aid organisation Christian Blind Mission International in 1998 when a freak accident left him a quadriplegic. After eleven operations, including one in which a doctor kept him alive by literally pumping his heart with his hand, Jim endured months of excruciating rehabilitation until finally settling into life in an electric wheelchair. So remarkable was his story that his spinal consultant called him 'Lazarus'.

One day I was just setting out with my dog Tyson for a walk when Diedre, the visiting spinal nurse, arrived. I greeted her from the footpath as she got out of her car. She suggested that we take a walk together while we talked.

We wandered around the corner and down a little court that led to a park. There I let Tyson off his lead to run around. 'We can sit over there under the shade,' I said, pointing to a spot under a tree. There was a log for Diedre to sit on, and of course I had my chair with me.

Watching Tyson and talking to Diedre, I completely forgot that the dog lead was still around my wrist and dangling on the ground. As we moved off towards the shade, the lead got caught in my back wheel. This pulled my hand down and my body forward, jamming my other wrist against the joystick that controlled the wheelchair. I couldn't release the joystick, so the wheelchair kept going, dragging me down even further as the lead got more entangled in the back wheel. Slowly I was pulled off the chair onto the grass.

Diedre watched in horror as I collapsed on the ground, my legs buckled beneath me. 'Oh no,' she wailed, 'now what are we going to do?'

I looked up at her and said, 'I dunno. You're the expert.'

'Well, I could call an ambulance, or go doorknocking for help,' she said as she arranged my limbs so that at least my body was straight.

'Don't call an ambulance,' I said, 'that seems a bit drastic.'

She straightened up. 'Well, do you have any other suggestions?'

'Can you see anybody around?'

'No, nobody.' All of a sudden she brightened up. 'I know, I'll quickly go back to the house and bring your hoist down.'

We had a portable hoist at home for lifting me, but the thought of Diedre dragging it through the streets seemed ludicrous. 'You're joking!' I said.

'No, I think that would be the easiest, quickest way.'

I saw that she was right. 'Okay, off you go,' I said. She ran down the lane.

I lay there staring at the blue sky. Suddenly I became aware that Tyson was beside me. He circled me, then without warning stepped over me and stood straddling my hips, his front legs on one side and his hind legs on the other.

'I hope you went before you came here, pal,' I said to him, then added: 'It's all right for you, you've got an electronic chip in your ear that can find you anywhere.'

He stood motionless and silent, looking down the court where Diedre had disappeared. It dawned on me that he was protecting me. He was standing guard—literally watching over me.

Tyson didn't move until Diedre reappeared at the end of the court, dragging the cumbersome hoist. Then he stepped off me and stood beside me, looking in her direction. His rear end was now in my face, with a dangling bit stuck to his thick, beautiful coat that I hoped was a bark chip. As Diedre came closer his tail began to wag, slapping me across the face.

Diedre put the body sling around me and lifted me into the wheelchair. Tyson yelped for joy; he knew I wasn't meant to be lying on the ground helpless. We must have looked quite a procession on the way home—Diedre first with the big electronic hoist, then me in my wheelchair, then Tyson tagging along faithfully behind.

And that, I realised, said a lot about the way my life would be from now on. There would always be traumas, trials, challenges, accidents, spills. I would repeatedly fall out of my chair and end up sprawled on the ground. I would always need help to get up and move on again. But somehow I knew the resources would be there when I needed them—just as Diedre was there, just as unexpectedly Tyson came through at the right moment. God would see to that. In fact, I thought, in a funny way God was a lot like Tyson. Whenever I was down, it was as though he was standing over me, watching out for me, hovering nearby until I could get up for myself.

And one day I will. One day I will get up and walk. One day I will be healed. One day the pain and suffering will be gone. I may have to wait until heaven for that day to come. But when it comes, boy, will God ever wag his tail! Will God ever bark with joy! Will God ever squeal with delight when I finally meet him face to face and he says, 'Come, my child, walk with me.'

Shout to the Lord!

Camerin Courtney

~

'I was actually embarrassed the first time I played "Shout to the Lord" for the worship pastor at Hillsong Church,' remembers Darlene Zschech. 'I made him stand with his back to me on the other side of the room! I'd play four bars and say, "I don't know if this is any good. Change whatever you need to." But he liked it, and the first time we sang it at church, people were on their feet singing along before we'd even gotten the words on the screen. It took off from there.'

Darlene didn't set out to write a globally popular praise song when she penned 'Shout to the Lord' in 1993. 'I wrote it when I was feeling discouraged,' Darlene explains. 'I felt I could either scream and pull my hair out—or praise God.'

At the time, Darlene and her husband, Mark, had two babies, and with a struggling motorcycle-parts business, money was tight. While Darlene and Mark revelled in their happy family, they also felt stuck in their financial hardships.

Darlene sang jingles for companies such as McDonald's, KFC and Diet Coke, and tried in vain with Mark to keep their business afloat.

It was during one particularly stressful day that Darlene snuck into the toy room where they kept their piano and put into song the spiritual truths to which she desperately clung: 'Mountains bow down and the seas will roar at the sound of your name', and 'Nothing compares to the promise I have in you'.

'Shout to the Lord' is now the most popular song in Australian churches and is sung by congregations worldwide. It has even been performed for the Pope at the Vatican and for the President of the United States. From humble beginnings, 'Shout to the Lord' has blessed millions and brought hope to the hopeless from Antarctica to Asia.

'The line "nothing compares to the promise I have in you" was something I clung to when our circumstances seemed so bleak,' reflects Darlene. 'I think that rings true with anyone going through tough times.'

The House With No Steps

Gordon Moyes

~

There is this guy I know who just inspires me. Don Campbell is a member of my Chapel in the City congregation, a lunchtime service held every Thursday. I have been preaching there for the past twenty-three years. Don is the first to tell you he's not much at anything. He's an alcoholic, though after years of drinking he's now sober. But he fears that even the slightest pressure will cause him to break down.

One night about twenty years ago Don's life was turned upside down when some drunk young men in a car were roaring through the Sydney suburb of Glebe. They were shooting at random at houses and a bullet passed through the shoulder of Don's son, smashing his spine and rendering him a paraplegic.

The Campbells were paying off a small narrow cottage in Glebe set high on solid rock. It was their dream house. But how could a paraplegic son cope with all the stairs? Don realised they faced enormous problems. But he had recently come to faith. 'God, somehow or other, you're going to make a new house here, a house with no steps,' he prayed. 'I'll start the job, but it's up to you, Lord, to finish it.'

Then he looked again at his house built on the rock and wondered. If they could get to the back of the house, cut away all the rock, they could extend out further and have everything on the one level.

The builders said it couldn't be done except at horrendous expense. The council inspectors said it was impossible. The social workers said the family would just have to sell and move to another area. But Don said, 'With faith in God, all things are possible.'

He purchased a large hammer, knocked a hole in the side wall of the house, put a tent around it to keep out the rain, and said, 'There you are, God. I've started it. I have no money or plans. I'm willing to work at it, but it's up to you to finish it.'

Don and his wife started with hammer and chisel chipping away at the rock. His knuckles were bruised and his arms weary as he carried away the rubble. The local Glebe newspaper ran the story and readers sent in $2000 to help.

One day a truck pulled up and the driver, unknown to Don, said: 'I've got some timber here you ought to have.' Then a builder, also unknown to Don, called in: 'I've got 200 bricks left over from a job. You can have them.' Next a couple from Ryde dropped in: 'Here are two special taps for the disabled, worth $80 each. You can put them in the bathroom.'

One day Don looked and saw that his patient chiselling had meant that all the rock was gone and the area was level. Then a call came: 'Can you use some concrete? I have a truckload we have to dump. Can we give it to you?'

'Yes,' said Don. 'Praise God, we've got the concrete! Bring it round.'

As he waited for the concrete, another unexpected truck pulled up and dumped yet another load of timber. The driver called out, 'Here's some more timber for you' and drove off, leaving the wood in the way of the concrete truck that was coming. Don despaired.

Then one more truck pulled up. The driver called out, 'You expecting some concrete?'

'Yes,' said Don, 'have you come to help?'

'No,' said the man, 'but I've got a message from the bloke who'll bring it. He's in a hurry and can't wait. He said he'll just have to dump the concrete and you'll have to move it. And watch out for rain. All day the radio has been saying that rain is coming. If it rains in the next two hours it'll ruin the lot. How are you going to get the concrete in with all this timber in the way?'

Don replied, 'I don't know. That's God's problem.' He remarked that it would take four men to shift the load.

The driver turned round and whistled. Three big Italian concreters jumped down out of the back of his truck. The driver said, 'Give us a hand to shift this timber round the back.' As they carried the last piece away the concrete truck arrived. But Don only had one wheelbarrow. He thanked the concreters as they walked back to their truck, but they had just gone back to unload four more barrows. Soon five barrows and five men were moving the concrete in. Within an hour they had even trowelled it up.

As they left, the driver said, 'You'd better pray it won't rain.'

'Well, it's God's concrete,' Don said.

For the next two-and-a-half hours the sun shone, and only then did rain. The concrete was safe.

Today that house in Glebe is called 'The House With No Steps'. What would have happened if Don had not started to build it? His family's wishes came true because they had faith, publicity, some good-hearted neighbours, and some kind-hearted workmen. But no one would have joined them if Don had not first of all knocked the hole in the wall and started chiselling the rock, working to make his wishes come true.

The Murrumbidgee

Michael Frost

~

I was camped on the Smith's property, Warangesda, a former Church of England Aboriginal mission. The derelict buildings and ramshackle windmill at the top of the rise above the river are the only reminder of its former use. Today, it's a rice farm.

When the sun goes down, the temperature won't drop until the early hours of the following morning. Swarms of screeching cockatoos sweep down the river gully at sunset. Their squarking can stop a conversation. That evening, at midnight, unable to sleep in the heat, I waded into the river and lay face up looking at the full moon above me. The current wanted to take me away so I had to anchor my heels in the sand beneath me and balance my weight against the flow. Even then I was dragged slowly, my feet leaving furrows soon filled in with river sand.

This was a moment I won't forget in a while. The yellow light of the moon flooded the river bank, turning everything sepia like an old fashioned photograph. The water trickling around my ears sounded like incessant baby talk. One old-timer had told me that this heatwave was the worst since 1939. Who can say? It was hot enough and the cool flowing Murrumbidgee, bringing water all the way from the Snowy Mountains, was our only saviour.

Why did I feel so aware of God's grace when I was lying in that river, when I don't sense it after turning on the air conditioner in my office? How come we feel so much closer to God on a headland overlooking the ocean than on a suburban street in a major city? The answer is because we know that only God could create so marvellous a thing as the Murrumbidgee River.

Never Give Up

Betty Cuthbert

~

I could feel the crowd saying 'they never come back' and it made me all the more determined to get up on top again.

The 1960 Rome Olympics were a great disappointment when injury stopped me competing, and I came away from them feeling that I just didn't want to face the constant clamour of public life any more. On the boat home I asked God whether I'd done enough with the gift he'd given me. I heard nothing in reply so I concluded it was all right to retire.

Gradually I stopped being noticed. The public began to forget what I looked like. I wasn't somebody out of the ordinary any longer.

Yes, I really enjoyed that first twelve months . . . but then a change took place. I began to feel I was drifting aimlessly. I wanted to do something more constructive. I tried a few things to keep me occupied, even ballroom dancing, but none of them suited me. I felt I was wasting my life.

One afternoon, about fourteen months after I retired, I was working in the nursery when it suddenly occurred to me that maybe I needed to take up athletics again. I thought: 'What a dreadful idea!' But I couldn't get it out of my mind. It was like a voice in my head that kept saying over and over: 'Run again. Run again. Run again.'

I fought that voice for two months. Eventually I couldn't sleep at night. I realised it was more than just an idea; somehow I knew it was God speaking to me. One night in my bedroom the voice said 'Run again' and this time I surrendered. 'Okay, you win,' I said. 'I'll run again.' Almost as soon as I said it, a strange and wonderful thing happened inside me. An amazing feeling that began at the top of my head and went right down to my feet washed over me. It was happiness: pure, delirious happiness. Suddenly I just *knew* I was back in the right niche, and from then till I did retire for ever after the Tokyo Games I was never happier in sport.

I trained hard and suffered many setbacks, and through the long, painful process my faith sometimes wavered. But I knew what I had to do and set my mind to accomplish it. I had my finest victory against great odds in Tokyo, but it wasn't just me. As I walked out to the track with the other runners all my normal nerves were gone. I felt totally serene. The starter's pistol fired and I shot out of the blocks, but I felt as if somebody else was running the race. And as I crossed the finish line, I was so certain that the victory was not just mine that I clasped my hands together quickly and said to God, 'Thank you.'

Later, when multiple sclerosis struck, I remembered those events and drew strength from them. Often I would call out to God for help and time and again it came along. I was so grateful that I had the experience of Tokyo to look back on. If God hadn't deserted me then, I reminded myself, why would he desert me now?

Balaam's 21st Century Ass

Phillip Jensen

~

'Then the Lord opened the donkey's mouth, and she said to Balaam . . .' Numbers 22:28

One of the privileges of serving Christ in Sydney today is the opportunity to share the great news of Jesus with people from all over the world.

It is a daunting task. But whenever we are overwhelmed we need to remember the sovereignty of God and that he can talk even through donkeys. It places our work in context and gives some realistic ground for optimism.

Ministry to overseas students is one of the greatest evangelistic and missionary opportunities for Australian Christians. Several groups on campuses around Sydney are seeking to reach these sojourners.

One such group introduced me to a man the other day whom I will call Fred. His name is hard to pronounce in English, but the reason I will call him Fred is that I do not want to indicate the country he comes from. Fred comes from one of those countries where news and media are censored. Where people live in fear of open communication. Where Christians are persecuted.

Fred came to study at one of our universities. It was a huge step in life for him. He already had a degree from a university at home. But by diligence and ability he had been selected to do postgraduate study overseas in Australia.

One of the first things he did in Australia was to find a Christian meeting. He met one of the groups on campus that ministers especially to overseas students. They provided a Bible for him and talked to him about Jesus.

'Have you ever heard of Jesus?' the leader of the group asked Fred.

'Yes. In a movie,' he replied.

Knowing that it had been translated into Fred's language, the leader asked, 'Was it the *Jesus* film?'

'No. Not a full length movie,' Fred replied. 'It was only a small part of a show. Actually it was a cartoon.'

'Which cartoon?'

'*The Simpsons.*'

'What did you learn about Jesus from *The Simpsons*?'

'Jesus died for our sins on the cross,' came Fred's reply.

Remember the sovereignty of God and that he can talk even through donkeys!

Parliament My Parish

Fred Nile

M y unexpected election to Parliament in 1981 caused me a great deal of heart searching. A number of my Christian friends criticised me for going into politics. They thought I was like other clergy who felt led into politics and resigned from the ministry as a result.

I responded, 'No! I'm different. I feel God has called me to exercise my ministry through the Parliament.' Parliament was my new parish.

Even so, doubts were planted in my mind, so I had to put God to the test. I was like Gideon, who put a fleece out three times to make certain the Lord was with him and would give him victory over the enemy. I prayed for the Lord to confirm that it was his will for me to serve him through Parliament by three clear signs.

The first sign came in a completely unexpected way. As I entered the Legislative Council for the first time, the attendant said, 'Reverend Nile, did you know this building was once a church?' I said, 'You must be joking.' 'No, it's true,' he replied. 'Look, I'll show you the original wooden shipment boxes.' They were hidden behind a small door in the chamber. Sure enough, the Upper House building had once been a pre-fabricated cast-iron Anglican church, built in Scotland and used on the Victorian gold fields. When the gold fields moved, so did the church. Finally, no longer required, it was put up for sale. The Legislative Council purchased it in 1856 for £1835.

So each day I sat in Parliament, debating and deliberating on bills and motions, I would actually be sitting in a 'house of prayer' provided by the Lord!

The second sign occurred on the first day of sitting. I had never been at the opening morning procedures of Parliament before and I found them very intriguing. The President entered and all the Members and the public in the visitors' gallery stood for prayers. The first prayer offered said: 'Almighty God, we humbly beseech Thee to vouchsafe Thy blessing upon this Parliament. Direct and prosper our deliberations to the advancement of Thy glory and the true welfare of the people of our state and Australia. Amen.' Members then said the prayer our Lord taught His disciples, the Lord's Prayer.

I discovered that the background to these prayers was highly significant. In 1547 the British House of Commons moved its meeting place from Chapter House at Westminster

Palace to the Royal Chapel of St Stephen, with all its ecclesi-
astical trappings. From that time too the Clerk of the
Commons began each day by reciting the litany. In 1659 the
first Speaker's chaplain was appointed to lead prayers. Then at
the first sitting of the New Parliament in 1688, the Puritan
chaplain prayed a prayer upon which our modern parlia-
mentary prayer was based.

This prayer and its modern equivalent were based on
Romans 13:1–7, which teaches that governments are God's
servants or 'ministers' to carry out His will on earth. This,
then, was the second sign from God. Truly Parliament was
God's 'house of prayer'!

The third and final sign concerned my discovery that I was
not the first ordained minister to serve in the New South
Wales Parliament. People criticised me for entering politics
on the grounds that I was somehow turning my back on the
ministry. When I checked the historical record, however, I
found that the original New South Wales Act allowed the
Governor to appoint five (and later seven) people based on
their senior positions in society to help govern the colony.
Among the original five was the Archdeacon of the colony,
the Reverend Thomas Scott. On 16 September 1829,
Archdeacon (later Bishop) William Broughton was appointed
to replace Mr Scott. So I was not the first minister in the
Legislative Council. God had prepared a seat for me as he had
for them.

25

So my request for three signs had been answered. There were no more doubts, just faith and trust. I strongly felt my shortcomings—many MPs were lawyers or university-educated and I had dropped out of high school at fifteen to work as a junior storeman. But I knew I had my seat in God's 'house of prayer' by his design.

I had another unusual experience that confirmed God was with me in Parliament. One day when first elected, I was walking through the Parliament House administration area where the Hansard offices are located and a senior Hansard editor came towards me. As he did so he raised his finger. I thought he was going to tell me off for being a busy body or ask suspiciously, 'What are you doing here?' Instead he said, 'I voted for you.' I was completely surprised. Fancy an experienced officer of Parliament voting for me, a complete novice! But he asked pointedly, 'Why are you surprised? You're like Elijah, who thought he was all alone and God rebuked him: "Don't you know I have reserved seven thousand men in Israel, all whose knees have not bowed to Baal?" [1 Kings 19:18].' Again I was encouraged to continue as God's servant in Parliament.

I still remember the loud-mouthed ALP Member who interrupted one of my first speeches. He kept interjecting, 'Anyhow, where is your parish?' I finally replied, as God gave me the words, 'Right here, brother! Right here!'

Lady of Leisure

Angela Eynaud

~

'et other pens dwell on guilt and misery. I quit such odious subjects as soon as I can,' wrote Jane Austen. I concur with her sentiments about misery, but guilt is something of an occupational hazard for Christians.

Take me, for example. I recently realised that if I were to sustain a job, volunteer at church and be available for my family I needed some time for myself or I'd go round the twist. I decided to work only four days and keep Fridays for me.

This was a surprisingly difficult decision to follow through. Initially I felt guilty leaving any task unfinished and would go to work all the same but not get paid for it. Other times I'd use my day being useful doing household running around—grocery shopping, cleaning and so on. No fun at all! So I employed a house cleaner. She needed the money and I needed the time.

Once or twice I managed to tear myself away and got in a few hours of serious shopping, but then I felt guilty for spending money unwisely in a world where some people are starving. I decided a better way to spend my time off might be having coffee and cake in a café and reading undisturbed for a couple of hours. Then I felt guilty for being sedentary and unhealthy.

I took my concerns to God in prayer, but prayer often makes me feel guilty because I don't pray often enough or feel the presence of God like I think I should.

Then I felt guilty for feeling guilty.

Why is the voice of self-recrimination so deeply ingrained that it defies all rational efforts to silence it?

As far back as I remember, I recall sermons and youth group talks encouraging, 'If God is going to convert the world he will do it through you. God's hands are your hands and God's feet, your feet.'

I was told if I shone as a light in the world people would be drawn to me and would ask, 'What is it about you that makes you different?' In my youth I dreamed of converting my entire secondary school, then leading a revival at university.

As the years passed and no one asked the question, 'What is it about you? I want what you've got', I began to feel uneasy about the effectiveness of my witness in the world. Far from flocking to my light, most people haven't been all that interested in hearing my life story and are amazingly complacent about their eternal destiny. I've found I am not so startlingly different from everyone else after all, just a fellow struggler.

This deeply ingrained impression that I should be busy saving the world has cast a shadow of unease when I enjoy myself. The persistent voice in the back of my mind tells me that there is always a more noble, more godly, less selfish way of spending my time, my energy, my money.

The problem stems from the language we use to describe the grace by which God offers us an opportunity to participate in his work in the world. We appropriate responsibility for seeing the job gets done and then lay the burden of the onus on ourselves.

God wants us free from guilt, revelling in the joy of being alive. Workaholism reflects a lack of confidence in God to realise his plans without our assistance. My inability to take a day off is in reality extreme arrogance. Do I think that because I am not at the helm God is hamstrung?

In future I'm going to enjoy my days off. And instead of looking over my shoulder to see if God is watching, I'm going to invite him along with me.

The Bus Fare

Pat Mesiti

~

Remember the little character Jiminy Cricket in the Walt Disney movie *Pinocchio*? He was the puppet's conscience who told him right from wrong. Unfortunately for Pinocchio, he rarely if ever listened to Jiminy and got into a lot of trouble. One pearl of wisdom from the likeable cricket was: 'Always let your conscience by your guide.' That's very good advice.

A friend of mine who is a Christian minister got on a bus one day after talking to a large gathering and paid his fare. It was one dollar. Mistakenly, the driver gave him back two dollars change. His first thought was it must be a 'provision from God', but then he decided to let the driver know of his error.

'Excuse me, but you've given me too much money.'

'I know I did,' replied the driver.

'What do you mean you knew you did?' came the bewildered response.

'I was in your meeting last night. I wanted to make sure you were the real thing.'

Decisions have a value structure and some values—such as family, marriage, trust and hard work—are not negotiable. They cannot be placed in risk. One of the things the great Indian leader Mahatma Gandhi taught was that conscience should come first and pleasure second. Pleasure without conscience is a recipe for ruin.

Jesus—Friend of Prostitutes

Tim Costello

⎯⎯∾⎯⎯

As a follower of Jesus of Nazareth, I had reason to reflect deeply on his friendship with those beyond the reach of civilised religious society: the publicans, prostitutes and despised tax collectors. The religious establishment of Jesus' time believed that if every Jew could obey the law for just a 24-hour period, then the Messiah would return, liberating Israel and instituting the reign of God on earth.

The ones thwarting this exciting prospect in the eyes of the doctors of the Religious Establishment were the very people Jesus included as his special friends. He was dignifying their immorality by being seen at their parties. His open company became a religious scandal, as he was holding back the righteous tide of history and the return of the Messiah. Little wonder these leaders started to plot his death. In their eyes, and by their criteria, Jesus was an unspeakable blasphemer.

Something of this gospel scandal was illuminated at a worship service at the House of Hope, a street-front community in St Kilda, in early 1994. The biblical text was the story of Jesus enjoying hospitality at the home of Simon the Pharisee. At the height of the feast, a woman of ill repute gatecrashed the party. She anointed Jesus' head with oil and wiped his feet with her hair. Stunned by this, the guests present and Simon the host expressed shock that Jesus' judgment was so bad that he, a religious teacher, had allowed himself to receive physical care from such a tainted woman. One could hear the audible gasps of shock from the righteous ones.

After the reading of this story, one of the congregation called 'Gay', herself a street worker in St Kilda, decided to comment. She was amazed at the courage of the biblical woman who risked total rejection. Gay said she had seen the parties on St Kilda Hill where BMWs pulled up outside Victorian mansions, letting out beautiful people dressed in extravagant clothes. They danced and partied in lavish style. She knew how dreadfully impossible it was for her to even contemplate gatecrashing because of the disgust that her presence would evoke. Her contribution to the discussion in the worship service on this biblical passage was what an incredible person Jesus must be to command such courage from a woman like her. What sort of love and acceptance did he offer that this woman in the Bible should risk social suicide and total rejection?

Gay's insight was profound and left all those in the worship service with a fresh way of seeing the meaning of the story.

She understood the text in its rawest, most direct form because she had put herself into the story. She was closer to the power of its liberation and truth than any of us from more respectable backgrounds.

The Body of Christ

Margaret Reeson

~

When Rabaul fell to the Japanese in 1942, Dora Wilson and other Australian nurses with the Methodist Overseas Mission, together with military nurses and nuns, were interned by the Japanese at the convent of Our Lady of the Sacred Heart at Vunapope on the island of New Britain.

It was like no other Easter they had ever known. Though the nuns had been given permission to attend Mass every day, this did not apply to the army and civilian nurses, and a number of them missed the comfort and strength of worshipping God together. To a degree they were confined to the convent and had little contact with the hospital, except through the army nurses, and no contact with the Australian men who were also interned at Vunapope except through messages carried by the New Guinean people.

On Good Friday morning Dora watched as priests, nuns and New Guinean Catholics processed into their cathedral. It was hard not to think wistfully of her parents and friends setting off for church at home in New Lambton and to wonder whether her mother had made hot cross buns this year. There would be no hot cross buns at Vunapope; the mission bakery supplied their bread, but with dwindling stocks of flour every slice of bread was precious and, if it had not been for the New Guineans' kindness in bringing food from time to time, they would have been very short.

Later that morning, accompanied by the other women, Dora walked quietly into the convent chapel. They had been invited to join the nuns for the Stations of the Cross. On one level she was very aware that this was very un-Methodist, alien to her upbringing, the aroma of incense and the succession of painted images of the road to the Cross unfamiliar. Yet in a deeper part of her this was known, rich with memory, part of her spirit.

The women moved thoughtfully and with prayers from one Station to the next, remembering the Christ who was betrayed, unjustly accused, threatened, beaten, mocked, made to carry a heavy cross till he stumbled and fell, crucified . . . Outside the chapel, enemy guards waited. In the mission grounds hastily dug graves hid the corpses of victims of violence. Once again, women waited at the foot of the cross, weeping for the pain of the world and for their own grief, waiting with the One who felt and carried the bitterness of a world in chaos.

An unexpected gift lightened Easter Day. 'Chaplain John

May has permission to come up to the convent on Sunday morning to celebrate Holy Communion with us! The priests have offered to loan him a mass-kit, with vestments, communion vessels, wafers and wine and everything,' the army nurses told them.

Early that morning the little chapel was dressed with fresh scented flowers from the gardens and the women waited for the young Anglican chaplain to come. They watched him walking through the garden to them, surprisingly without a guard, and heard young New Guinean children calling greetings, 'Happy Easter, *Masta*, Happy Easter!'

They were all there, Kay Parker and her army nurses, Joyce Oldroyd-Harris and the nurses from Namanula Hospital, Dorothy Maye in from Kavieng, Mrs Bignell, Dorothy, Chris, Dora and Mavis. The chaplain and his prayer book were Anglican; the chapel and the wafer on their tongues were Roman Catholic; the women receiving the eucharist were Methodist, from other Christian churches or from no church. But for these believers, there was a strong sense that Christ was alive among them, that dawn would follow darkness, that hope could defeat despair.

The Ballad of the Two Sons

Kel Richards

⁓

(Luke 15:11–32)

Near the town of Bundiwallop,
Where the sun sets in the west,
Was a sheep and cattle station
By the name of 'Come-and-Rest'.

Sam McPherson was the owner
(A top bloke—the best of men)
And Sam was Dad to two sons:
One was Dave, the other Ben.

Now Dave, he was the older,
Made for work and not for fun,
While Ben was lighter hearted,
He was Sammy's younger son.

One day when in the home yard
Sam and Ben were dipping sheep,
Ben asked his Dad a question
That knocked Sam in a heap.

'Dad, I know you'll die one day,
You'll tumble off the twig,
And I'll inherit half the property
And a chance to make it big.

'Well, Dad, you know the truth is
I'd rather have it now.
You see, I wanna leave the farm
And forget the sheep and cows.

'I wanna hit the big smoke, Dad,
With some dough I can invest.
Dad, I wanna get away from
This farm called "Come-And-Rest".'

'But, son, I thought you liked it here'
Was all his Dad could say,
'Cause Ben's request had sort of
Taken Sammy's breath away.

Reluctantly Old Sam said, 'Yes,
Let Ben his fortune seek',
And gave Ben all the paddocks
To the west of Snakebite Creek.

The stock and station agent
Came and did a deal with Ben,
Brought a contract for the paddocks,
Ben whipped out his fountain pen.

Ben packed his clothes into a port,
In his wallet put his dough,
Shook hands with Dave and hugged his Dad,
Then turned his back to go.

Ben ended up in Sydney,
Where he opened an account
In one of the better known banks,
With a fairly large amount.

But the money ran though Ben's young hands
Like water through a sieve,
He made some flash new city 'friends'
Who said: 'We'll show ya how to live.'

Eventually Ben found his way
To a place they call Kings Cross,
And being rather naive,
What he thought was gold, was dross.

Ben's brain just overheated,
He rioted and rambled,
He fell in with the wrong crowd
And drank and drugged and gambled.

His new friends gathered round him
Saying, 'Ben is great, we think.'
And that is what they all said . . .
When Ben was buying drinks!

Eventually the dough ran out
And every buck was spent,
And Ben just couldn't figure out
Just where the money went.

Wherever all that money went,
It had certainly shot-through.
And when the money ran out,
Ben's 'friends' all did so too.

And at the very moment,
Just to make things more depressin',
The national economy
Collapsed in a recession.

So Ben began to hitch-hike,
With his swag his only load.
Ben went back to the bush again:
Looked for work upon the road.

Eventually he got a job
At a dingy little farm.
They hired Ben as pig-man,
A job without much charm.

They didn't pay or feed him much
As he sloshed about the sty.
Ben said, 'These pigs are eating
Much better food than I.

'I'm working in this pig-yard
Where I slop and feed and dig—
Why, I'm just another animal,
Just a vertical pig!

'The stockmen on Dad's station,
Back home on "Come-and-Rest",
Are better off than I am;
Perhaps I should head west.

'I'll go back to my father.
I'll say: "Dad, I got it wrong,
I turned my back on you and God,
Turned my back for far too long."

'I'll say: "Dad, I know I've given up
The right to be your son,
So I'll come back as a farm hand,
If you can use an extra one".'

So he went. He passed through Bundiwallop,
Then he climbed the last steep hill,
And in the distance spied a figure,
Someone waiting for him—still.

Through the dust that always blows about
The western slopes and plains,
Ben saw a waiting figure
Beside that dusty, outback lane.

The figure ran towards him,
Ben saw it was—his Dad!
Old Sam he wept, and Ben wept too,
They wept from feeling glad.

Then Ben he said his piece:
'Dad, I know I got it wrong,
I turned my back on you and God,
Turned my back for far too long.'

But Sam gave Ben a great big hug;
He could barely speak for tears.
The only words that Sam said were:
'After all these years!'

Sam found his best Akubra
And put it on Ben's noggin,
And gave him brand new leather boots
(His own were worn out sloggin').

Sam took him back to the homestead,
To a farmhand said: 'Hey you!
Go and kill that poddy calf,
It's time for a barbecue!

'The one who was dead is now alive,
This is my boy, my Ben,
My son who was completely lost,
Has now been found again.'

Now the stockmen liked their boss, Old Sam,
And they shared the old man's joy.
And, truth to tell, they quite liked Ben,
And were pleased to see the boy.

So they killed the calf and butchered it
While the western breezes blew,
And they built a fire and gathered round
And began the barbecue.

One bloke was missing from the feast,
He was out on the edge of the run,
Mending the boundary fences.
That was Dave—Sam's elder son.

As Dave rode back to the homestead,
He could hear the laughter and song
Carried upon the dusty wind
And thought: 'Now what's going on?'

When Dave rode into the home yard
On his big black gelding horse
He was told, 'Your brother Ben's come back,
So we're having a barbie, of course.'

Dave went all quiet and sulky
And muttered, 'So that's what it is.'
He refused to go into the party
And worked himself into a tizz.

Sam came out to talk to Dave,
And Dave said, 'Dad, be fair,
I've slaved away like a navvy,
And sometimes I think you don't care.

'You never said to have my friends
Around for a barbecue.
You never offered to give me a feast
Of a scrawny chook or two!

'I'll bet my brother wasted his dough
And it ran right through his paws.
I reckon most of it ended up
In the hands of Kings Cross whores!'

Sam grabbed Dave and gave him a hug,
Saying, 'Son, you're always here,
And I do appreciate the fact
That you never cause trouble or tear.

'But the one who was dead is now alive,
Your brother is back, our Ben,
My son who was completely lost,
Has now been found again.'

Comfort or Convictions?

Steve Grace

～

There's a question each of us will have to challenge ourselves with many times in life: where do you draw the line between your comfort zone and the convictions of your character?

We rolled into town past the famous Premier speedway track to the wintery sights of Warrnambool on the rugged Victorian coast. There was a bitterly cold southerly wind blowing in off the ocean, but it didn't dampen the enthusiasm and expectations of the local church folk who were waiting to welcome us to town. This was a relief as I could sense my team were road weary. As we backed the truck into the loading dock at the performing arts centre, I knew already it would be good night. And it was. A near capacity crowd filled the auditorium and the band performed well. We were halfway through a long tour and fatigue was beginning to wear us down. But nights like this always give you the stamina to keep the dream alive.

From there we were heading north with a dozen towns to visit on the 2400 kilometre journey home.

God always seems to put the right people in your path when you're worn out and weary, and he did again on this occasion. After the truck was packed, we all drove to the home of a caring family for a late meal and some rest. They lived in a beautiful old two-storey Victorian manor with ornate furniture to complement the era. The chilly conditions outside were soon forgotten as we entered the dining room to a long table fully prepared for a feast. Silver cutlery, decorations and the aromas drifting in from the kitchen affirmed in unspoken words that we were appreciated for our work that day. There were big servings of beef stew, chicken and vegetables, homemade apple pie and cream. Long into the night, the hospitality, laughter and fellowship filled the home of this kind family. I quietly wished every town had families and accommodation like this.

The next day we all slept in, then after a five star breakfast we burned up some energy out on the tennis court next to the swimming pool. This was my kind of property. The family was in the process of completely renovating the old home, but we didn't really notice. We felt like kings for a day. Our clothes washing was done for us, our appetites over filled and the stresses of touring life eased.

But all too quickly attitudes can change. We farewelled Warrnambool and headed north to a smaller rural town that was doing it tough. The colourful coastal greens soon faded to parched browns and the musty haze of drought. When the land is suffering and dry, the people are usually harder to connect with. The local pastor in this town was still very grateful to see us. He had worked hard to get some willing help for this event. Apathy has a stronghold in so many Australian communities. Even finding accommodation had been disheartening. When the pastor had asked for help, only one person had made their home available—a young single mother on welfare who had recently become a Christian. She'd arranged to move out for the night so our team could all stay.

Wrestling with the reality of another set up, we were all indifferent to the task ahead. Our leisure day off was over. It was back to work. The concert did not go well. The crowd was down and quite unresponsive. To be honest, it reflected our attitudes and expectations of the event. In life you get what you give, but the guys and I were in no mood for any wise counsel. We loaded the truck and made our way to our arranged accommodation.

On entering the rundown and tired place of our lodging, we were confronted with the ugly stench of cat litter—and, on finding the light switch, a house in shambles. Old magazines and plastic K Mart toys covered the floor. The TV was dead and there was hardly any food in the fridge. A cloud of murmuring and complaint filled the atmosphere. Lukewarm showers in a mildew-covered bathroom did little to alleviate the mood. No one was speaking. My thin mattress on the floor in a cold room, which I shared with my sound man, Geoff Bentley, was well worn. I sprinkled eucalyptus oil on my pillow to create a presence of hygiene. I couldn't wait till morning so we could get out of there and on the road.

Then at 5.30 a.m. I woke with a deep sense of conviction. I looked across and Geoff was laying there with his eyes wide open. I knew he was thinking the same thing. We were wrong, all of us. God did not bring us to this house to fill it with ungratefulness and pride. He arranged this visit to check our hearts and hidden motives. We were becoming selfish and conditional, losing touch with the needs of the very people God had called us to relate to through our concerts.

Without hesitation we woke the team. Our challenge to get up hit home through bleary eyes. They too recognised their failings and negative attitudes. We prayed together, then after a coffee to kick start our brains we planned some action. We would turn this grungy house into a home. Everyone took on different duties and rooms, and when the supermarket opened we got some food supplies, chocolates and flowers. I was proud to see my mates being so domesticated. The toilet, laundry and kitchen sparkled. I autographed some CDs and placed them with a card on the dining table.

By 9.00 a.m. we departed, each smelling of ammonia and detergent. Each knowing we had won a personal victory. Each knowing always to be grateful in every circumstance.

The Battlefield of the Mind

Margaret Court

~

Had I known back then what I know today about the power of words, I would have won six Wimbledons, not just three!

After my inexplicable 1961 Wimbledon loss as the number one seed in the first round, the media saw my nerves as my Achilles heel and proceeded to exploit this fact on every possible occasion. There was no way they were going to let me forget my mistakes. Every year they turned up in full force to see whether the 'Aussie Amazon' could finally overcome her centre court jitters and take home the coveted trophy. Headlines screamed from the sporting pages, CAN SMITH EVER WIN WIMBLEDON?, effectively destroying the small amount of confidence I had developed from winning every other Grand Slam title in the world. Sometimes, when I went out in ordinary clothes and no one recognised me, I would hear people talking about me, not realising I was standing in front of them. Comments such as 'I don't like the way she plays' or 'She'll never win' were not the words I needed to hear.

Every year I came in as the No 1, fit, strong and well-prepared, just as I was for every tournament. Yet Wimbledon always remained my bogey tournament. The difference was not in the physical preparation but in the mental arena. I tried desperately to put all the negative words from my mind. To win I had to believe 100 per cent that I could do it. But I knew there was that small area of fear, placed there by those negative words, lying just beneath the surface of my outward composure.

I never had a problem with any tournament in the world except Wimbledon, because no other press in the world was as savage as the British press. While what others say about us is powerful, however, even more powerful is what we say about ourselves. It wasn't just the negative words of the press that caused me such problems at Wimbledon. It was the fact that too often I secretly echoed those words myself.

If we are told often enough that we are useless, hopeless, stupid or good for nothing we will eventually start to say the same things about ourselves. The more we say, the more we will believe those soul-destroying words. And when we believe them, we will fulfil them to the letter.

Even in tennis my battlefield was often not the court but my own mind. When I believed I could win and said as much, I usually did. But when I believed I couldn't and said as much, I always lost. We say such bad things about ourselves: 'I'm ugly',

'I'm dumb', 'I'm lonely', 'I'm sick', 'I'm depressed', 'I'm a failure', 'My hair is always a mess'. Instead we should say: 'I'm beautiful', 'I'm lovely', 'I'm successful', 'I'm a winner', 'I'm smart', 'I'm righteous', 'I'm healthy', 'I'm happy'—all the things that God says we are. For God created us, and he doesn't make junk!

Tears of God

Michael Frost

I heard an associate of Australian evangelist John Smith tell a story about the day Smithy was presenting a religious education seminar in a high school in Melbourne. After the formal input, the students were invited to put any questions they might have about religion or Jesus or Christianity on cards to be read out on the platform and answered by John. Most of them were serious questions about the sensibility of the Christian faith. But one of the questions read, 'Where was God when I was raped?'

It is a theological question. But it was also a cry from the heart. After it was read and before John Smith could answer, he began to weep. His friend who told me the story said big salty tears rolled down Smithy's cheeks into his moustache and for several seconds he couldn't speak. The whole group of students fell deathly silent as the evangelist cried on the platform for the pain expressed in the desperate question on that card.

There was no need for any theological answer after that. Where was God when I was raped? The answer was expressed in those big, salty tears.

The Newcastle Freeway

Gordon Moyes

Once I was driving from Sydney to Newcastle. At 6.45 a.m. I was at Swansea when I saw a green plastic garbage bag stuffed with garbage by the side of the road only a metre from my wheels. I thought it must have fallen from a truck, but as I drove past a casual glance revealed an astonishing sight: a legless bare pair of men's buttocks sticking out the open end of the bag, covered with blood.

I couldn't believe what I had seen. It couldn't be! There was no room in the bag for a body, unless it had been cut up. I drove on, shaking my head, thinking that in the early morning light I was seeing things.

Then I stopped. I was not seeing things. I turned the car round and drove back.

It was a pair of bare human buttocks. They were stiff and cold. But there was no bulge in the garbage bag where a head should be. I thought I had found the remains of a dissected corpse.

I carefully rolled the bag over to see if there were any legs. There they were, curled up inside the bag in a foetal position.

The rest of the body groaned and moved.

He was a 25-year-old man, severely battered about the face and covered with blood. He was lying where he had fallen after being pushed out of a moving car while drunk. During the night he had crawled into the garbage bag to get out of the rain. At one stage, curled up tight inside the bag, he had pulled his trousers down to relieve himself. The blood on his buttocks came from his own fingers as he tried to pull his trousers up.

I pulled the garbage bag off and checked if he was all right. How he did not suffocate with his head tucked under his arm at the end of the bag I do not know.

He immediately swore at me and threw a punch at my face. Then he argued with me to leave him where he was. I helped him off the road into the bushes where he pulled the garbage bag over his head again.

I drove off to go to my speaking appointment at a businessmen's breakfast, feeling rather relieved. But I was not happy. So I drove back again, and found the man still curled up inside the garbage bag. I called to him to get out and helped him up. He threw another punch at me.

'You're the second person to wake me up!' he said.

I pushed him over to my car, intending at first to take him to hospital. Instead I took him with me to the Apollo Motor

Inn where the businessmen's breakfast was being held. I was met by a surprised waiting crowd. In the gents' toilet I helped him clean up, dropped his soiled underwear into a bin and dried him off under an electric hand dryer. I took him upstairs and introduced him to some of the men as my friend John. He had several cups of black coffee to sober him. Some of the businessmen surrounded him with interest and support.

As I was talking that morning about how society does not really see the homeless, he stood up and interrupted me. He wanted to tell his story to the whole assembly. He was homeless. He had been retrenched as a ladder maker and had gone to find a cheap caravan to live in near Newcastle in the hope of finding work. He had a wife and six-year-old daughter somewhere in Sydney. They had been separated since he lost his job.

He explained how he had ended up where I'd found him. He had been drinking with friends until a fight developed and they dumped him bleeding by the side of the road. He sheltered from the freezing rain in the garbage bag. I had called him out of the bag, which had almost become his tomb.

And in fact, I reflected as I listened, he was almost as good as dead. Unless his life changed, he was headed straight back into the tomb—be it in a caravan or a garbage bag. Unless he turned to Christ, he was dead. Only Christ could give him life.

The Christian businessmen in that area determined to continue to help him, until he was in a clear mind and they could present the claims of Christ to him. One offered him a job in an aluminium extrusion factory doing the work for which he had experience. Members from a local church arranged a caravan for him and his wife and child to live in as temporary accommodation until something else turned up. The family eventually became members of that church.

Jesus met a young man on his way to the cemetery at Nain (Luke 7:11–17). He was dead, but Jesus gave him new life. It happened again on the Newcastle Freeway!

Sunday Night Live in St Kilda

Tim Costello

Arrogant though it sounds, our study of the gospels suggested that the middle-class church did not necessarily know much about Jesus of Nazareth. His inclusivity and scandalous friendships with social outcasts was an offence to normal notions of decorum. It was in the schizophrenic and psychotic that we discovered that the friendship of Jesus is for all. The good news of a loving, transforming presence in a callous world is for everyone, not just the beautiful who have capped teeth and professional careers. It is for all of humanity. Communion as an open table symbolises this conviction.

I remember one Sunday night cringing at the messages people had grown up hearing from the church. When the cup was being passed around, Kevin, who had just started coming, blurted out, 'Can I take communion? I am a bad man and have done time in prison.' He was encouraged to partake with the words that all of us fail God and ourselves and we all need the forgiveness that communion expresses.

Just at this point, one of the women we grew to know and love, an Aborigine called Eva, piped up. Turning to our ex-convict, she enquired, 'But wait on, love, have you had sex before marriage?'

He understandably looked a bit shocked and responded, 'Oh yeah, but what about everyone else here?' I noticed the rest of the congregation got rather itchy eyebrows, or at least they started rubbing them furiously, staring down at the floor. Most seemed relieved to treat this as a rhetorical question not demanding any further confessional candour. The cup was passed to Kevin and he took it and longingly drained it. He was so impressed that he exclaimed, 'Not a bad drop.' And for our diluted grape juice, that's saying something.

To some, this may read as a trivialisation of the most sacred meal. To us it was a penetration of the gospel that people named sins. For street people, the 'sins' they felt the church would pin on them were these very matters such as time in prison and indulging in premarital sex. How could those with sexual peccadillos or criminal prior convictions be included in the communion of saints who were welcome at the Lord's table? Yet the old book depicted these very tainted people as the ones with whom Jesus shared table fellowship.

Table fellowship in Semitic culture was no casual business lunch where you settled a deal and moved on. It was a major social statement of profound proportions. You only ate with those whom you were willing to have publicly identified as your closest friends. Jesus mixed with the wrong crowd. Our middle-class training had taught us well that you are known by the friends you keep. Strangely enough, we were being liberated in St Kilda by a few modern-day examples of the friends of Jesus.

So communion became an open invitation, without a fencing rail and pastoral checks of communicants' prior convictions. I remember a Christian policeman coming to a packed evening service and showing signs of public discomfort throughout the service. He was stationed at St Kilda police station and rushed up to me after the service requesting that we speak privately. In an agitated tone he said, 'There is something you must know', and then he discreetly pointed out five people that he knew had been charged or arrested over the previous weeks and related their various suspected offences.

I waited patiently for him to finish and politely thanked him for his concern. I simply asked him if he was pleased that they were in church. He looked shocked, then sheepish, and rather quickly excused himself. I have a hunch that Jesus would not blanch at such company.

We encouraged a sharing of personal struggles so the church might prayerfully support them at every communion service. Sometimes, this was like inviting an unguided missile attack.

One particular evening, a natural street poet was at church. He had suffered a massive breakdown at university and was later diagnosed as suffering from schizophrenia. Life became a series of transient boarding houses and seedy hotels, with annual admissions to hospital to stabilise him on different forms of medication. His pain and burning hope to be well was brilliantly verbalised in his poetry. That night in the sharing time, he shocked most by unblushingly asking for forgiveness because he had had a woman that week. Someone well intentioned but tactless unhelpfully chimed in, 'Well, at least it wasn't a man.' After the initial stunned silence at his frankness, people gathered around, laid hands on him in solidarity and love, and prayed for him.

The letter of James in the New Testament exhorts us to confess our sins to one another. But in all my years of church attendance, I had never heard anyone take this that seriously. This act of self-exposure opened all of us to deeper levels of confession and truth-sharing. And once again, it was the street folk who led the way.

You've got Mail

Phil Gibbons

～

My wife Jan and I 'met' via a Christian match-making website and started e-mailing each other in July 1998. We soon discovered we had a terrific amount in common. The more we wrote, the more we discovered we shared—likes, attitudes, foods, musical tastes. Everything! On top of that she was intelligent, had a great sense of humour and, most importantly, was a full-on Christian.

I had been praying for several years that God would lead me to the right woman to be my wife. I must admit that I was beginning to wonder if anything would ever happen. Now things were looking up. We were e-mailing each other up to three times a day and often talking on the phone.

Before long we agreed that we should swap photos. I definitely liked what I saw, and apparently so did Jan. The fact that she lived in Texas and I lived in Mackay, Queensland, didn't seem to be anything that couldn't be overcome if God was in the relationship.

It was time for some serious praying to find out if Jan was indeed the right woman for me. I asked God to show me in some unmistakable way—and soon!

The next day I heard a song called 'Midnight Train from Georgia' on the radio and one of the lines really grabbed my attention: 'I'd rather live in his world with him, than in mine without him'. I thought to myself, 'I wonder what Jan would think about that if she heard it?'

Later that day, when I checked my e-mail messages there was one from Jan. 'Guess what, honey,' she wrote, 'I heard this song on the radio coming home from church yesterday. It was "Midnight Train to Georgia" and the girl said, "I'd rather live in his world with him, than in mine without him." Although it sounds like she's making a sacrifice, it would be no sacrifice to me because that's how I feel. I'd rather live in your world with you, than in mine without you.'

You could have knocked me over with a feather. I'd wanted an answer and I'd got one! Jan had no idea what I'd been praying the day before, yet we both heard the same song at the same time, and both picked up the same words. It was especially neat that it was through music, because we both love music so much.

Jan was very brave, I thought, to come all the way out from Texas at Christmas so we could meet for the first time. For all she knew I could have been some weirdo stringing her along. But unbeknown to me, God had reassured her, again through a song, that 'I would be right there waiting for her' (a Richard Marx song) and everything would be fine.

To say it was fine is an understatement. We clicked from the first minute. Jan returned home two weeks later with an engagement ring on her finger.

On 10 April 1999 I married Jan, my beautiful wife, hand-picked from heaven. How special is that? To know that God looked all over the earth, found the right two people, arranged it so we'd meet, and then confirmed to us both that we were right for each other. Neither of us has any doubts about this. We are blown away by God's goodness to us.

What Will I Give My Kids?

Glenn Williams

~

We had just heard the news from the doctor that Mum had only a short time to live. The daily visits to the hospital would soon come to an end. The pain of seeing her suffer would soon be over, and the unbearable grief would soon take its place. Oh, how we would trade it all to have Mum back with us.

After receiving the news from the doctor that night, my dad and I walked to our car. I will never forget what happened next. Dad put his arms around my shoulders and said, 'Son, God's plans for us don't stop here because Mum is going to be with the Lord.'

The memory of those words spoken in the midst of such pain and sorrow only reinforces for me the reality of my parents' faith and reminds me of the rich heritage I have to pass on to my children.

To this day I vividly recall the many nights I held my son, comforting him and settling him to sleep, wondering how many times my own mother did this for me. As I prayed for my son, I wondered how many times my mother prayed for me. Sometimes when my son cried my heart would break—how many times did I break my mother's heart?

Before I became a dad I could never imagine how much love a parent could have for a child. But now, as a father, the deep love I have for my son helps me to fathom a little of the love my mother had for me and how difficult it must have been for her to eventually say goodbye to her family in those final moments. I want my children to know that same love. I want my children to share in that rich heritage I received.

Dr James Dobson shares a story about how one of his close friends collapsed and died on the basketball court while they were playing together. In the moments that followed, he thought about his own mortality. 'What if that had been me?' he wondered. Would he be happy with the legacy or heritage he would leave behind? Two words came to mind—'Be there'.

The following day he sat down with his seventeen-year-old son, Ryan, to share his thoughts on this circumstance. He said:

We all must face death sooner or later and in one way or the other. And, of course, it will also happen to me. I don't know if I'll have an opportunity to give you my 'last words' then. So let me express them to you right now. Freeze frame this moment in your mind, and hold onto it for the rest of your life. My message to you is Be There*! Be there to meet your mother and me in heaven. Don't let anything deter you from keeping that appointment.*

Dr Dobson wasn't saying his son's accomplishments were unimportant, or that he should not aspire to reach his potential. He was merely trying to highlight that these things pale into insignificance when compared to being there for eternity.

If you're a parent, perhaps one of the most important questions you might ask yourself is: What sort of legacy or spiritual heritage will I leave my children? Here's how you can give your children a strong spiritual heritage:

1. Start by identifying three things you wish you had received from your parents that you didn't, and contemplate how you can go about giving these to your children. You might want to talk to a trusted friend, pastor or counsellor to help you do this.
2. It's very easy to let the busyness of life cram out the things that are really important. Make up your mind that you won't use this as an excuse, and plan time out with your children by putting it in your diary as a non-negotiable appointment. If you can't keep it, don't cancel it—reschedule it.

3. Many things start with a vision. Prayerfully ask God to give you a vision for your marriage and family. Then start planning some realistic goals that can be reached in the short-term that will move you closer to that vision. Don't start too big, otherwise you'll set yourself up to fail and possibly never try again.

4. Be willing to parent out of your weakness. To constantly feel as though we need to have all of the answers and never let our children down will only lead to disappointment and unfulfilled expectations. Be honest with them about your fears, anxieties and mistakes. Let them know what you are learning from them. This gives them the confidence to know you will love them even if they fail.

5. Introduce some important communication boundaries for your home. Be careful to expect the same standard from yourself as you do from your children. Don't raise your voice or yell at each other. Don't criticise or put each other down. Don't call each other names. If something has upset you, work out a time and place where you can sit down and discuss it—wait for the heat to die down first. Be willing to negotiate some agreed consequences for over-stepping the boundaries.

6. Build into your family routine those things that will free you up to grow your relationships. Only have the television on at certain times of the week. Eat a meal together at least once a week (without the TV on). Plan one activity

every week or month where somebody else in the family gets to choose what they want the family to do.

7. Establish family traditions. Plan to celebrate each other's birthdays and make sure everybody is home to participate in the event. Where possible, involve friends to show them that this is a time where you honour the person whose birthday it is. Family and friends can make this a very special event in the life of a person. This can become a time to be greatly anticipated by all.

Overcoming Fears

Ken Duncan

When I'm travelling in America, people often pick up on my accent and tell me they would love to come to Australia but they believe we have too many dangerous animals. It's true we do have a few nasties, but they rarely bother you unless you do something silly. For example, if you swim in areas inhabited by saltwater crocodiles, then you could have a problem on your hands—or on any other part of your anatomy those primeval monsters take a liking to! But if you take reasonable care and show a little respect around crocodiles, you're fine.

Crocodiles don't venture far from water, they can only run fast in a straight line on land, and they don't climb trees. Not so the American grizzly bear! That animal is one keen, mean fighting machine—not only can he run faster than a horse, but he can also swim and climb trees. It seems the only thing he can't do is fly, and that's not much comfort because neither can I!

73

I went with a friend into Denali National Park in Alaska to photograph Mt McKinley. In preparation for the trip, I tried to find out as much as possible about mountain biking, backpacking and camping out in bear country and how to deal with any other hazards we might encounter. All the people I spoke to kept drawing my attention to one thing—grizzly bears! One well-meaning adviser told me that if they run at you, they might simply be testing to see if you run. So, whatever you do, you shouldn't run. (Apparently bears like to play chicken!) He went on to say that if the bear keeps running, you should curl up in a ball and play dead. If he keeps attacking, then you must fight back. What a fine thought—hand to hand combat with a grizzly. I know who I'd put my money on! On and on went the horror stories about people being mauled by bears—even dragged from their tents—and many people suggested we should carry a gun.

It's amazing how fear can creep in and try to stop you fulfilling your destiny. Fear can be healthy in certain situations—like preparing us for fight or flight—but that nagging worry of 'What if a bear comes?' can be a total waste of time and energy. Sure, it's good to have knowledge—I have learned that preparation helps avoid desperation—but in the end the journey must go on and it doesn't make sense to let fear put fences around our dreams. We must trust in something bigger or we will always be living in the smallness of our emotions.

I told our informant we would put our trust in God and he would look after us. In the end we settled for bear bells and decided we'd make as much noise as possible on our way through the park so as not to surprise a dozing grizzly.

Although we had no problems with bears, we did meet up with another of Denali National Park's infamous residents. We had just finished shooting a full moon at sunrise over Wonder Lake. (Wonder is the perfect name for this lake, as the beauty of God's creation touched me deeply and it is an experience I will always carry in my heart.) We had made our way back to the bikes, and I was just strapping the tripod onto the carrier rack when I saw my friend—his eyes as big as saucepans—looking over towards another small lake and mumbling something. He was making weird hand signals, sticking his thumbs in his ears and wiggling his fingers. Then, in exasperation, he just pointed to the lake.

I looked across and got his message straight away. 'Moose!' I yelled. 'Yes,' he shouted in reply, 'and it's huge!'

He jumped onto his bike and took off as the moose came thundering towards us. With one eye on the advancing moose, I secured the tripod to my bike rack and then started pedalling to catch my friend. Thanks to a bit of healthy fear, I pedalled like I've never done before—my legs were going like pistons—and I didn't look back again until I reached the top of the hill. Fortunately for us, the moose stopped halfway up the hill. People told us later that moose can be more

75

dangerous than grizzly bears and proceeded to relate a string of horrific moose tales.

To me, life is a lot like that. We can spend an enormous amount of time worrying about the bears that may come and trying to anticipate every twist of fate. But often, in the end, it's not the bear that comes at all—it's a giant moose!

When You're Going Through Hell, Don't Stop

Pat Mesiti

◦∽◦

A thousand conflicting thoughts and emotions ricocheted around inside my head and tugged at my heart. I looked up at the man who sat beside my hospital bed in silence reading a newspaper, his sarcastic smile saying, 'I've got one over you, Mesiti!' He hadn't said a word all day. It was another one of his ploys to degrade and humiliate me.

What was going on? Here I was at the tender age of twenty-four, in my first youth leadership role since graduating from training college, a total emotional mess. The victim of verbal abuse, ridicule and unjust accusations; of being told day after day that I was an embarrassment, a hopeless speaker, a nobody who would never amount to anything. And there was my leader, a dictatorial, mean-spirited, cynical and hurtful man, enjoying every minute of it.

I though of my young wife, Elizabeth, at home in our ramshackle, falling-apart house with our first newborn, Rebecca. I knew Liz was worried about what would happen to me—not knowing what lay ahead or whether I still had a career or not. I had already endured a childhood with alcoholic parents, going through constant shame and insecurity, but this was worse. This was hell on earth.

I had firmly believed my lifetime destiny was to make an impact on young people, but nothing had prepared me for this. Was it the end? Would I have to quit? Go and find an office job? Give up my passion to change lives?

Everything in me wanted to reach out and scream. I wanted to call my family and order some customised concrete shoes (I'm Italian, you know). Anger wanted to rise up, reason tried to squash it down, confusion ran round and round. My brain felt like it was in a blender.

In the middle of this pain and uncertainty I made a very important decision. Today, with the luxury of more than ten years hindsight, I can clearly say that one thought changed my life. It made me the man I am today, relating to hundreds of thousands of teenagers and businesspeople each year.

What was the decision? I remember saying to myself: 'I will refuse to get bitter. No one will have the privilege of dictating to me how I will respond. I am going to keep sweet.'

Bruce Springsteen had a song that went 'Like a river that doesn't know where it's going I took a wrong turn and just kept going'. That's a tragedy. Life shouldn't be like that.

I eventually made it through that horrific episode and my youth work progressed. Was it easy? No. Did it take time to heal? Yes. But the important thing is I made it. I moved on to build the Youth Alive movement and speak into the lives of people all over the world. And I believe I'm a better person for it.

This pre-Promised Land experience, as I have since called it (because it felt like I was all alone in the wilderness), taught me a very valuable lesson. When it feels like you're going through 'hell on earth'—a totally horrific experience—don't hang around. Don't even slow down. Keep on moving out of there as fast as you can. Look for the exit and run!

My destiny was far too important to surrender. My desire to help people meant everything to me. I had no Plan B to fall back on. It was this or nothing. So I put up with the ridicule and torment, got myself out of hospital, and concentrated on building an effective youth movement.

And what happened to the other guy? He hasn't been heard of since.

Dream House

Angela Eynaud

❧

Quite regularly we receive mail advertising a raffle where first prize is a grand home, usually on the Gold Coast. The houses rarely hold much appeal for me. They are invariably huge, pastel palaces decorated blandly in cream or beige and looking so much alike that it would be hard to recognise yours from the neighbour's.

But last month the house was different.

Firstly, it was perched on top of a hill with views to distant mountains. There was a grand sweep of lawn and established trees. The house was sandstone with wide verandahs, white posts and a grey roof. Inside, it was painted in warm colours with dark polished wood furniture and trimmings. In the bathroom there was a claw-footed bath! The *pièce de résistance*, however, was the round music room with the cathedral ceiling.

I drooled. I dreamed. I coveted. Then, like Eve, I dangled the temptation in front of my husband. He looked. He drooled. We dreamed together. Imagine if . . .

Then the phone rang. It was the house raffle company asking whether we wanted to buy a ticket in the draw for $10. We bought four.

Over a cuppa we sat down, confident of our imminent win, and began to discuss the impact the acquisition of our dream home would have on our lives. Within five minutes we were arguing.

'We're agreed we'll shift to Queensland then?'

'But our families are here.'

'There's plenty of room for visitors.'

'Of course we'll sell the house after a short stay and use the money to finance the ministry of our church.'

'Over my dead body. You're not selling my house.'

'What about the kids' education?'

'Come on, they'll love Queensland!'

And then I realised what I'd done.

Some time ago we'd paid off the mortgage on our home. Almost immediately the pressure came from all quarters to put our house on the market and purchase a bigger home in a 'more desirable' area. With two incomes it was economically possible. It certainly seemed to be the way other people were going: buy, renovate, make a profit, buy a second home, repeat the process. One by one the other mothers in the playgroup sold up and moved to 'better' suburbs. I began to pressure my family to make the move.

We nearly did it, until we realised we actually liked where we lived, felt called to the church we attended and were happy with our children's school and our jobs. The choices we had made and the life we had built together were good. To take out another housing loan would put an end to the opportunities we wanted to offer our children—swimming, music and dancing lessons, and visits to museums, the theatre and the zoo. It would limit the money we had available to support missions and our church and to give to the poor. So we gave our house a new coat of paint and stayed.

And yet the materialistic lie that life is about constructing the best standard of living you can afford still worms its way in when I'm not looking. Here I was, wasting $40 on raffle tickets that might win me a home I didn't really want. As I contemplated life in my gorgeous dream home miles away from friends and family, without the pressures of work and church, I realised how awful it would be. An empty music room, a claw-footed bath I'd rarely use but have to clean often, and a heart heavy with the knowledge I'd run away from the life God had given me and the job he'd called me to do.

We know our kind Father won't give us a snake when we ask for a fish, but what does he do when his children ask him for pretty snakes? I trust he knows better than I and that I won't win that house.

A Boy and a Kangaroo

David R. Nicholas

~

O nce I was walking along an Australian bush track with my small son. It was early morning, the mist still hovering close to the ground. Looking up, I saw a kangaroo on the track ahead. It stopped for a while, stared at us intently and then bounded away. My son couldn't understand why it was in such a hurry to leave. We walked on without seeing the animal for quite a while; then, two or three bends further along the track, I caught sight of it again.

'There's the kangaroo,' I whispered.

Not at first seeing it, my son shouted excitedly, 'Where, Daddy?', immediately startling the elusive creature, which hopped out of sight.

I tried unsuccessfully to convince one small boy silence is golden when you are looking for a kangaroo. I realised we would not see it again that morning. The noise had sent it away.

In the middle of life we sometimes wonder why God does not seem near. The heavens appear as brass. We seem cut off from God. Has the noise of life been the cause?

God can and does speak to us even in the middle of life's noise. However, we need to prepare ourselves in the quiet so we can live better for God when we are surrounded by distractions.

Isaiah had the same trouble back in his day. The people found it difficult to hear God's voice, so he counselled, 'In repentance and rest is your salvation, in quietness and trust is your strength' (Isaiah 30:15b).

The Day God Burst Out of His Box

Geoff Bullock

~

Jesus and his disciples were on their way home to Galilee. To travel from Jerusalem in Judea to Galilee they had to pass through Samaria. They were on the journey home and were tired and hungry, so they stopped for lunch at Jacob's well in the Samaritan village of Sychar. They had every intention of continuing. I can imagine the disciples calculating the time spent for lunch and working out how much travelling time they had left in the day. They were probably aiming at a town further down the road where they could stay for the night. This little stop was just a break to eat.

You know the feeling. The bags are packed tightly into the back of the car and you're barrelling down the highway, carrying a small gang of hyperactive back-seat terrorists. When they start to get dangerous, the peacekeeping force—one female negotiator and one male sharpshooter who doubles as driver and transport captain—decides to think about a quick lunch. Instead of a well, you pull up at one of the major 'Service Centres' that punctuate interstate highways at intervals of every two hours (about the range of a small child's bladder). As you arrive at this designated 'terrorist feeding site' (usually marked by a large yellow M), the peacekeepers inform the terrorists: 'You'd better hurry up, we have a long way to go. Make sure David and Phillipa wash their hands. Where are David and Phillippa? Maddy, go and tell David that the big truck has a very big driver who may not like his artwork on the truck door. No, we can't have sundaes. And where are the teenagers? Why can't teenage boys keep their eyes off our teenage girls? And hurry up! I wish we'd left earlier. Get back in the car. Don't argue about it, we'll sort it out when we arrive. No, no, yes, a long way. Go to sleep. No, we won't be listening to *that* CD. And if you don't shut up now I'm turning around and going home!'

I am sure that you have been there. The last thing on your mind is making conversation. The last thing on your mind is striking up a friendship. The positively last thing on your mind is staying for two days.

Jesus and his disciples were 'just passing through'. He had no intention of staying. He was on his way home.

Jesus sat by the well. He was probably hungry. We already know he was tired. It was the middle of the day. He was hot, dusty and (enter Samaritan woman) thirsty.

When a Samaritan woman came to draw water, Jesus said to her,
'Will you give me a drink?'

The first question we should ask ourselves is, Why was this
woman coming to the well in the middle of the day? Surely
the women of the village would have gathered around the
well in the early morning to draw water for washing, breakfast and their husbands' cups of tea. They would have returned
in the cool of the evening to get water needed for the evening
meal, the dishes and cleaning teeth. This little gathering of the
village women would have been a very social affair. All the
latest gossip would have been told, retold and exaggerated.
Who was going out with whom, who was having a baby,
whose husband had been seen with whose wife, whose
children tormented whose lamb—a real Samaritan *Who*
magazine, without the pictures! So why was this woman there
alone? Surely she would have preferred the company of her
friends.

Maybe she wasn't interested in all the gossip. Then again,
maybe she was the gossip.

Picture the tragedy of this poor woman's life. From the
minute her first marriage started to fall apart she was
sentenced to the shame of failure. I can imagine that every
new marriage brought new hope. Then, slowly but surely,
every new marriage brought the same problems, the same
sense of growing helplessness, the same tragic decline, the

same mind-numbing loneliness. Five men, five marriages, five failures, until she didn't have any courage left. Now she was living in a de facto relationship rather than commit herself to another painful eventuality.

Jesus was not waiting by the well for his disciples to return. He had sent them away so he could be alone. Alone with his way of doing things. Away from their questions and moralising. Away from the pressure of having to explain himself. He was waiting for an appointment that had been arranged from the very beginning of time, an appointment that would stand as a testimony to God's unconditional love, acceptance and grace. An appointment that would broadcast to the world of broken lives that stretched out in time from this well side a testimony of hope and restoration.

Jesus was waiting for the moment to reveal his heart, and therefore the heart of his Father, in such a way that, if people would just dare to understand and believe what he said, God would never be thought of in the same way again. God was about to burst out of his 'box'. Yes, after Jesus' crucifixion, the curtain in the temple was torn, signifying that God had now made the way open to all. But here, at Jacob's well in Sychar—in despised Samaria, of all places!—God was about to personally rip up the veil that covered a broken woman's heart.

The Great Maladikarra

Dave Andrews

~

believe that in every culture, tradition and religion, in every part of the world, there are types of Christ—Christ figures who, somehow or other, prefigure the spirit of Christ—to whom we can turn, and who, in turn, can point us towards the person of Christ himself.

George Rosendale, a respected elder from Hopevale, an Aboriginal community in far north Queensland, says that in his culture the Christ figure was someone called the 'Maladikarra'. He writes:

> If someone is before the Aboriginal law court, and is condemned to die, the way he is to die is by being speared by his people. When he is to be speared, he has the right to get a defender. In my language we call him—'Maladikarra'. The Maladikarra 'speaks for the one that is in trouble'. If he cannot persuade the court to stop the spearing, then the Maladikarra stands in front of this other man, between him and the fifty or sixty people who are

89

going to spear this man. The Maladikarra says to this man, 'All right, don't watch the people, don't watch the spears, only watch me. Watch my movements. Whichever way I move, you follow my actions.' They don't throw the spears one at a time. They throw them whenever they wish. Five or six spears come at one time. The Maladikarra has to stop these spears. He knocks the spears away with his Woomera. He does this until all the spears are broken. When this is done, the man is free. The Maladikarra stakes his life to save this other man.

'There is a tremendous message here,' says George. 'It is the message of Christ. He is the great Maladikarra.'

All Before Lunch

Sue Duggan

~

oday is the first day that I have moisturised my face in nearly two years.

I brushed my teeth for the first time in eight days, answered the telephone without shaking and was civil to the man at the door who was trying to sell pay television. This is the day that I got out of my pyjamas-cum-tracksuit and put on street clothes. I even had the courage to look at myself in the mirror. It is the day that I showered and blow-dried my hair, put the children in the car and returned the library books that were twenty-five months overdue.

Then I blew it.

I set myself up for this particular fall after watching an episode of Oprah—a heartening show called 'Turning Your Trauma to Triumph'. All the guests were women who had faced terrible loss and whose lives had been shattered. They came to Oprah's attention because they chose not to sit on the ash heap of their circumstances. Instead they turned their lives around and fashioned them into something terrific. Each person could remember, and describe vividly, the defining moment when they had decided to take control and take back all they had lost, and some.

I was an easy convert. My whole body reacted to the sniff of a quick fix. My problems seemed petty in comparison. Probably because I still label myself and not my illness, and I tell anyone who asks that I am around the twist. In my corner of the world, that means that depression and all its scurrilous little cronies like anxiety and panic reside at my house.

I should have recognised the pattern, but I did not. I drove to the library wondering why I used to believe that getting my act together on the spot was impossible. It did not occur to me to congratulate myself for getting dressed. No, I muttered unkindly to myself as my body began to flag and let me down. Eventually, around lunchtime, I could not ignore the ache in the muscles at the base of my neck any longer. I did not recognise all the signs that pointed towards a state of rising anxiety.

I pulled into my driveway, heart beating and head thumping, and so I was not as vigilant as usual. I headed for the mailbox without thinking or even checking for the enemy. Any adult human. I am particularly wary of meeting my neighbour, partly because there is an unresolved dispute between us but mostly because I'm scared of my own reactions. Since the day I decided my home was to become my entire universe, I never *ever* go to the mailbox without first checking.

If you don't think about it too hard, that was my first big mistake.

The mailbox held only one letter. It was from our local council. Our neighbour had complained again. I threw my head back and groaned. Then, at the same time that I noticed my hands were shaking, I looked up and saw him not three feet away.

There are pros and cons to being sanity-challenged. I have lost many of the social niceties that I used to have down pat, but in their place I have developed a new power of knowing what other people think when *I* am scared. This ability kicked right in. The man looked smug. In that same moment of clarity, I knew too that my best strategy would be to turn away and start work on my new Oprah-style life. Instead, I let those little fingers of fear do the walking and I irrevocably ended up in a space marked 'hyperventilate'.

We had a full and frank discussion which was enjoyed by most people in the street and probably anyone who was listening in the next suburb. My neighbour threw insults. I, on the other hand, had the good grace to throw only facts! When he ran out of insults and was sure his audience was paying attention, he brought out the big guns.

'Call yourself a Christian? Call yourself a Christian?'

I withered. Fell at the first hurdle. I was much too anxious and embarrassed to give him a good answer. I wanted to say something that was totally politically correct and, of course, revealed God in all his glory. Instead, I could only blurt out what was true for me.

'Yeah, I am a Christian and, believe it or not, it's what keeps me sane. It's *because* I'm sick and *because* I lose my temper that I go to church. And, in case you're wondering, the reason I go twice on Sundays is I'm not perfect yet.'

With as much condescension as one man can muster, he told me to get off his property.

So much for a life of triumph. I ran into the house, bolted the door and howled. What a great advert for church I have turned out to be. I felt like the whole world was laughing and the angels were just shaking their heads in disbelief.

I blew it.

On days like today, I believe God is going to drop me like a sixth grade romance. I find it much easier to fear his anger than remember his love. Then I fuel all my anxieties by wondering what displeases him the most. Is he angrier because I dumped on my neighbour or because I stayed home from church to watch TV and eat chocolate while yelling like a tyrant at the children?

Just quietly, I think he will be sad because I thought I could change myself without his help. I have been crazy long enough to know exactly how much he loves me. Nothing I said today even comes close to some of the things I have thought in the last couple of years, and he has heard it all. He loves me patiently.

He knows I need understanding and encouragement by the truckload. He knows too that I am not very good at reciprocating when I find it. Best of all, he knows what that translates to in my shaky little world. I am selfish, lazy, square-eyed, fragile, introspective and egocentric.

What *I* know is that he would never use these words to describe me.

He is my friend, and I have not spoken kindly to him in a long time. Even so, he waits. It takes a while to heal a wounded spirit.

How Do We Choose Our Heroes?

Mal Garvin

∽

*D*o you have any heroes?

If we asked an American who his national heroes were, he probably wouldn't have any trouble giving the names of any number of presidents and American folk heroes.

But who are our Aussie national heroes?

By any measurement us Aussies are a funny lot. In our hall of fame, there's not many great talkers or philosophers. No, the ones we remember are those who didn't give in to unreasonable authority, who excelled as sportsmen, who took mateship seriously. In the Aussie hall of fame we find characters like Ned Kelly, Don Bradman and Simpson, the man with his donkey.

Simpson was born in England and came to Australia when he was seventeen. He quickly picked up the bush lore—how mates worked together—and he loved it. It was as if it was already under his skin. He may have been born an Englishman but he became, like many after him, Australian by choice.

A lengendary Australian, one with a pride in his new country that few could exceed.

In her book *Anzacs*, Patsy Adam-Smith wrote this of Simpson: 'There had to be a hero, the people demanded one. So there was a hero, but this one was different. This was a man as redolent as a gum tree; as Australian as a kangaroo; a real colonial sprite. He'd scarcely begun his task . . . he was dead before Australia knew he was alive.'

What did Simpson do to become such a hero? Here's how his CO put it:

'He discovered a donkey in a deserted hut, took possession of it and worked up and down the dangerous valley that was called Shrapnel Valley. He carried wounded men to the beach on his donkey. It was such a great success he continued day by day from morning to night and became one of the best known men of the Division.

'Everyone from the General down seems to have known him and his donkey which he christened "Murphy".

'The valley at the time was very dangerous as it was exposed to snipers and also continuously shelled. He scorned the danger and always kept going, whistling and singing. He was a universal favourite. He worked like this for three weeks.

'On the night of 18 May the Turks made a heavy attack on our position. Early in the morning, as usual, [Simpson] was at work when a machine gun played on the track where he was passing. . . . He fell on the spot, shot through the heart.'

On the morning of 19 May he went up the valley past the Water Guard where he generally had his breakfast, but it wasn't ready. 'Never mind,' he said, 'Get me a good dinner when I come back.' He was never to come back.

What makes this story even more extraordinary is something only discovered after his death.

'Enquiry discovered that he belonged to none of the AAMC units with his Brigade. He had become separated from his own unit and had chosen to carry on his perilous work on his own initiative,' wrote Colonel, later General Sir John Monash.

In camp before he had left Australia, Egypt and, at last, Gallipoli, they all said, 'He was a man to have beside you when the whips were cracking.'

Yes, Simpson understood what it was to be a mate—to even lay down your own life for the welfare of others.

Psychologists believe that we often admire in others what is already there, but still unborn, in ourselves. When we look in the reflection of our heroes, what do we see? We see a people not ashamed to come from honest, ordinary battles; a people who are sensitive to justice, love and freedom.

Simpson's choice to leave safety and self-interest to take his stand under our Red Cross for the sake of his mates gave the land of the ordinary people an ordinary hero.

And it also etched into Australian history the echo of another man who also rode a donkey, a man who gave up his life on a cross to declare a Kingdom of Goodwill.

Perhaps a long-eared donkey instead of a bunny would be a better Aussie symbol for the true meaning of Easter.

The Day the Creek Broke Its Banks

Kel Richards

❧

(Matthew 7:24–27)

They were mates and they were neighbours—
Bluey Banks and Clancy Stone.
They'd often meet down at the pub,
Or natter on the phone.

Their stations were adjoining—
Two nicer farms you couldn't seek.
The dividing line between them was
A stream called 'Lambing Creek'.

Blue and Clancy and their families,
Decided they would build
Themselves two brand new houses,
By the creek, not on the hills.

To the north of Lambing Creek
Clancy's fancy slowly rose,
Upon a shelf of solid rock
Above the water where it flows

But Bluey built *his* dream house
On a sloping, sandy flat,
Even closer to the water—
On a beach is where it sat.

And when their homes were finished
On their verandahs they could stand,
And call out to each other
Across the water and the sand.

One day the clouds grew blacker,
Rain thundered from the skies.
It teemed and poured and pelted—
Then the creek began to rise!

The creek became a river
And the river roared and ran.
It surged and rushed and rattled—
More a lion than a lamb!

The wind blew through the gum trees,
It whistled and it screamed.
The sort of weather Noah knew—
Or that's the way it seemed!

The creek was like a living thing,
A full-on foaming flood,
A roaring, raging monster
That was out for human blood.

The wind whipped up waves wilder
Than humans ever saw.
Those waves demolished Bluey's house
And smashed it on the shore.

Then though they lashed and crashed about,
Those waves could never reach
Clancy's house upon its rock,
High above the beach.

And when the storm had faded
And the creek had gone back down,
The house built high on solid rock
Was still there—safe and sound.

The Religious Fifth Column

Fred Nile

~

I t was at the United Faculty of Theology in Sydney that I first encountered what I came to call the 'Religious Fifth Column' in the church. This Fifth Column was hard at work undermining the faith of the students who were training to be ordained.

The students came from the Methodist, Presbyterian and Congregational denominations, and many had experienced a definite evangelical conversion and calling into the ministry. Yet the very gospel which had saved them was ridiculed and rejected by the majority of the professors. The students came saying, 'I'm not ashamed of the gospel of Christ, for it is the power of God to salvation for everyone who believes' (Romans 1:16). They left with their beliefs in tatters. One student, who had been converted in an evangelical tent mission, said to me just before he graduated that he would do all he could to destroy tent missions. Another student lost his faith completely and told me he was resigning. I asked him what he was going to do. He replied, 'I've applied for a job as a barman on the Gold Coast.'

These students had been brainwashed by the constant attacks, lecture by lecture, day by day, week by week, on the Christian faith, and especially attacks on the trustworthiness and value of the Bible. The lecturers often denied the fundamental truths of the gospel. They claimed the virgin birth was a Greek myth—that Mary was only a young maiden, not a virgin, and must have had sex with Joseph, or perhaps a Roman soldier. They said Jesus did not die for our sins—the blood doctrine was based on Egyptian and Persian ceremonies in which converts were bathed in the blood of a bull. The resurrection of Jesus was not a physical, historical fact. There was no such thing as 'conversion'. Every miracle could be explained away—God did not part the Red Sea, the Israelites walked through the shallows; Jesus did not walk on water, he walked on a wharf and only *looked* like he was walking on water. On and on it went—lie after lie, blasphemy after blasphemy. No wonder many ministers today have no power or conviction in their preaching, or resign from the ministry with nervous breakdowns and other problems.

I fought these lies in every lecture. God was putting me through a spiritual and intellectual toughening up course. If I could survive this barrage I could survive anything. I had to write two answers to every examination question so I could pass and graduate—the answer they wanted from the modernist textbooks, then the truth from God's Word, the Bible, and evangelical scholars.

Eventually, despite all the obstacles, I finished my five years of study. When I went to discuss graduation, the principal said, 'I'm sorry—you have to do another year of study.' I was shocked and asked why. He said, 'Because of your Bible knowledge.' I pointed out that Bible subjects were my highest marks—an average of 92 per cent. He replied, 'No—it's because you still believe the Bible is true.'

So for another twelve months I experienced intense small groups and tutorials as the teaching staff tried to destroy my evangelical faith.

But, praise God, they completely failed. In due course they had no choice but to reluctantly graduate me and approve my ordination. I received the Licentiate of Theology, the basic qualification to be an ordained minister, and also completed the examinations for the Diploma of Religious Education of the Melbourne College of Divinity. Their plan to make me change, make me give up, make me resign had failed.

Hiding God's Word in My Heart

Barry Chant

~

I am forever grateful for the people who taught me to memorise Scripture when I was a child.

My mother died when I was ten years old. A few months later, no doubt to get me off his hands for a while, my father sent me to a Scripture Union boys' camp at Victor Harbor, a popular holiday town in South Australia. I was actually two years too young to attend, but because of the circumstances they allowed me in.

The speaker at this camp was a wonderful children's evangelist named A.H. Brown. His story-telling ability was legendary. If I live another fifty years, I shall never forget his breath-catching, heart-stopping narration of the tale of Nebuchadnezzar's fiery furnace. And I am sure I shall never hear anyone tell it better.

On Sunday night night we all went to the local Church of Christ for the evening service. Mr Brown was the preacher. He spoke on John 3:14–15:

Just as Moses lifted up the snake in the desert, so the Son of Man must be lifted up, that everyone who believes in him may have eternal life.

He told a dramatic story about an old medieval manuscript which depicted the people of Israel in the days of Moses trying desperately to save themselves from a plague of venomous desert snakes. Some struggled, others prayed, some relied on helping their suffering neighbours, others tried to flee—and all failed. But those who simply looked at the snake on the pole were saved. And so Mr Brown invited us to look to Jesus.

I sat at the end of one of the church's unusual slatted pews, stirred by this simple, vivid message. Young as I was, I felt impelled to stand to my feet. I did. I looked. And I was saved.

Looking back, I can see that the little Baptist church I was attending at the time had many weaknesses, but they did teach me some powerful principles. 'If you want to grow as a Christian,' they said, 'you must pray and read the Bible every day.' To be honest, I didn't always do it! But sometimes I did. They introduced me to Scripture Union notes. These were of enormous value. Through them I discovered some of the great evangelical authors, whose writings also were to stand me in good stead. In recent years, it has been my privilege to write for Scripture Union. This has been a special joy.

Then, at the age of fourteen, I was baptised in the Holy

Spirit. What an impact this made on my life! It seemed that I could hardly get enough of the Word of God. I used to rise at six every morning and pray and read the Scriptures. In summer time it was a pleasure; in winter it was not so easy! I can still remember huddling over my little table in my cold sleepout (the only heating we could afford in our home in those days was the kitchen stove and a small kerosene heater in the lounge room, neither of which was of any help to me), wrapped in overcoat and gloves, with a woollen scarf around my neck, studying the Bible and wrestling with God in prayer.

Somewhere I found a small red-covered notebook and wrote reflections on my reading each morning. I ended up with a commentary on the whole gospel of Mark. Over the next couple of years, I did the same with John. I tackled Revelation next—but that proved rather more difficult, as did the minor prophets. Nevertheless I struggled on. I kept and treasured those notes for many years—although I confess I never read them—until, to my sorrow, they were destroyed in an office fire in 1987.

There was only one other Christian in my class at my high school, but within two years we doubled our numbers. We used to pray together at lunchtimes and encourage each other.

Then, in my sixteenth year, I transferred to another secondary school, and found myself in a large class of forty-eight boys, eleven of whom were Christians. What a year we had! We weren't very popular with the others, but we certainly made our presence felt. We made a covenant with each other that every school day we would learn one verse of Scripture by heart. Taking a clue from a missionary speaker who visited our lunchtime prayer group, we labelled the memory verse a 'WT'—a 'wondrous thing' (Psalm 119:18, KJV). Each day, as soon as we met, we would challenge each other to quote our 'WT'. That year we learned the whole of Romans 8 and numerous other passages by heart.

Later, at university, we continued the practice of exhorting each other to regular prayer and Bible study. I remember confessing to a friend one day that I had missed my Bible reading. 'How could you miss it?' he asked in astonishment. I was so ashamed that I kept it up without a break for a long time after that. Today, the value of that regular input of God's Word is immeasurable. How grateful I am to God that he brought the right people across my path to encourage me in learning it by heart.

In recent years, I have continued to try to memorise Scripture. I have also tried to do it accurately. Many people know the Bible in an untidy way. The verse they want is half-way down the page, in the first part of the Bible, underlined in green, just near a thumb-smudge. This is fine as long as we have our own Bibles! I discovered that accurate learning of Scripture means knowing chapter and verse as well and being able to find a text in any edition of any translation.

Moses said, 'These commandments that I give you today are to be upon your hearts' (Deuteronomy 6:6). David wrote, 'I have hidden your word in my heart that I might not sin against you' (Psalm 119:11). I thank God that I learned these principles while I was young enough to derive the greatest value from them.

Missionaries Use Their Feet

Phillip Jensen

～

The motor car is one of the great inventions of humanity. It places within the reach of most people the capacity to travel huge distances relatively quickly, cheaply, in great comfort and with sense of personal freedom and control. The car enables us to travel door to door on our own timetable.

There are disadvantages to car travel, like pollution, traffic and parking—but most of these are community problems rather than personal disadvantages. For some regular trips commuting by public transport is cheaper and more convenient, but in general it is hard to persuade people to give up travelling by car.

However, it was in visiting a 'carless' missionary family overseas that I saw the gospel disadvantage of car travel. Everywhere we walked together, people greeted my friends. They would introduce their friends from Australia and would talk briefly of cabbages and kings. I cannot repeat the conversations because of the language barrier. The conversations were inconsequential and even trivial—but they were the building blocks of relationships. Our missionary friends were well known and liked—they were part of the neighbourhood and community.

Visiting a park we became engaged in a serious conversation with an elderly man about life and philosophy, about the Second World War and his family, about his joys and disappointments in life. It was natural and easy—because conversation was natural and easy. Sharing something of our faith was easy in such a context.

It made me reflect again about our treasured motor cars. Driving out of the drive, waving only at the next door neighbour, we travel in the splendid isolation of the radio community. We know more about what is happening on the other side of the world than the other side of the street. We know the names of the families of the stars better than the names of our nearest neighbours.

The car gives that sense of control that makes us rush—without time to stop and chat. Walking by its nature takes longer and is more easily interrupted by the reality of humans we meet and pass, or even travel with. It is like the two people who were walking and talking on a seven mile trip from Jerusalem to Emmaus. Fifteen minutes by car and no interruptions from strangers!

Part of the difficulty of evangelising in a modern city,

especially in areas of high rise housing, is the problem of having no point of contact with the community. It is not our problem alone, for the community no longer has much contact with itself. The car is not the sole villain in the piece, but it was interesting how in the 2000 Olympics the same openness to conversation happened as on the mission field. Strangers engaged in friendly conversation in the street like the old days.

The mission field I was visiting was more high rise and urban than most of Sydney. The car was as universal there as it is here. The difference was the missionaries' efforts to talk to people as they walked around their neighbourhood.

The Fear of God

Michael Frost

❧

'Aren't we meant to fear God?' Well, it depends what you mean by *fear*. We know fear to be terrifying and repulsive. Fear drives away. Fear creates anxiety and thereby it limits, retards, paralyses and destroys. Is this how we are to approach Jesus?

Come on! Of course not. What the Bible means when speaking about the fear of God (and similar phrases) is best translated by our English word 'awe'. To hold something in awe is quite different from being afraid of it. Fear repels, but awe attracts.

We see this in the way children respond to those things they hold in awe. My wife and I often take our children to Manly for an ice-cream and some fun on a Saturday afternoon. Manly is a Sydney seaside suburb with a large plaza which is usually packed with tourists and locals enjoying the beautiful, sunny concourse. It is also littered with buskers. Once such busker who is often there does a routine where he climbs on top of a two-metre-high unicycle and juggles fiery torches. He also makes jokes as he does it, so he has to yell at the top of his voice in order to be heard.

There he is with no shirt on, bathed in sweat, screaming his head off, balancing precariously two metres in the air and hurling fire overhead—pretty frightening scene for a three-year-old. But how does our three-year-old daughter react? It is a scary spectacle, but what does she do as he performs this bizarre routine, ringed by a jostling crowd of onlookers? She moves *closer*. Not too much closer. She wouldn't dare draw near, but she is attracted to the spectacle. Her mouth hangs open and her gaze is transfixed. She leans forward and slowly edges towards him. This is *awe*.

According to His Purpose

Gordon Moyes

～

In mid–1975, while ministering at the Cheltenham Church of Christ in Victoria, I had a strong conviction that the church should purchase the large double block of land and house at the end of Pine Street, a street that divided our very extensive property. I wanted this house and the large double block for the church to build a child care centre. We had four young children at the time, and it seemed, with over 300 children in our Sunday school, that a day child care centre was what was most needed.

The need was simple: we wanted to bring glory to God by serving the needs of the community. The problem was, we had extended our property enormously and had no money in the bank at all. We had just finished building a large retirement village near the church and had purchased several houses for demolition for the building of a further retirement village. We had assets but no cash!

I stood on the road, faced the house and the double block

of land and prayed: 'Lord, I believe you want this land for the development of our church—to minister to the needs of others. I claim this land now for your work. Thank you for giving it to us!' As I stood in the middle of the road I felt really stupid. With no money in the bank, it was to all intents and purposes a foolish prayer.

I thought laterally for answers. One was to get the Whitlam Government to buy the land and house for us. I approached the Children's Commission to get a grant to cover part of the cost of a huge child care complex. Eventually a grant was promised. We were excited. Then everything went wrong: Gough Whitlam was sacked on 11 November 1975. The Fraser Government stopped the grants. The Children's Commission was closed down and we could not purchase the property. It was just as if our prayers had been in vain and God was allowing us to be mocked!

We then discovered that one of our elders, George Daff, was related to the lady who owned the property. She was his wife's aunt. So we commissioned George to negotiate with her. We agreed on a price, placed a small deposit, and arranged that when she was ready to sell we would borrow and pay her the remainder. We rejoiced at how God had enabled the plans to be worked out.

Soon afterwards, a man stood at the door and handed me some money. It was the wealthy builder who lived over the back fence from the property. He gave me back the money we had placed as a deposit and simply told me he had made a surprise cash bid for the house and it had been accepted. The papers had been signed before we knew it.

A wave of anger swept over me. God had let us down. We'd been robbed. I looked hard at him: 'Damn you, Bill Marshall! You knew we wanted that land and house to minister to others. You would have read that in the church paper your kids took home. And knowing we'd put the deposit down and were about to sign the papers, you went in and confused the old lady with cash and pushed us out!'

The builder looked coldly at me. 'I bought it for my daughter to live in. You'll be marrying her in a couple of years, and we want her to live next to my wife and me. Sorry about your plans, but in this life cash always wins.' We had no cash so Bill got the property. He then rented it out for a couple of years until his daughter was married in our church.

I had wanted that property for the right reason—to help children in need. But we soon discovered our plans had been for the wrong age group. The great need of our area was not child care but aged care. Before long we had over a hundred people on the waiting list for our Christian Retirement Centre. We had two centres and opened a third, but the waiting lists grew even longer.

Then, two years after the night the builder told me he had brought the property, he was once more standing on my doorstep. 'I've got a problem,' he said. 'You know I've been renting out that property at the end of Pine street. Well, it's brought me nothing but trouble. The first crowd in there were all drunks who threw their bottles over into our swimming pool. Then there were those motorcycle people who repaired their bikes in the lounge room. Then it was those young people with the rock band and we couldn't get a wink of sleep. And now it's my daughter; she and her husband don't want to live so close to us!'

He paused and took a deep breath. 'I'm not going to rent it to anyone else. I'm wondering if the church would do a deal. I'm short of work at the moment, and I know you have a lot of people on the waiting list to get into the Christian Retirement Centre. If you gave me the contract to build another retirement centre for you, I'll give you the land—free! You could lease the units so it wouldn't cost you any money, and you would own the property without it costing you a cent.'

Carefully controlling my words and trying not to appear too eager, I replied, 'Well, I'll get our people to consider if we still want it.'

I had prayed for a ministry on that block. Now we got the house, two large blocks of land and a purpose-built two-storey brick building to complete our ministry to the aged—and the whole project was completed without the church having to borrow or raise a cent!

I couldn't help but think of the assurance I had forgotten

when everything went wrong: 'We know that in all things God works for the good of those who love Him, who have been called according to his purpose' (Romans 8:28).

Lessons from the Street

Tim Costello

~

Our church motto was 'committed at the core and open at the edges'. In St Kilda, this required very open edges.

I had grown up with the maxim that cleanliness was next to godliness. I had heard it so many times when growing up that I assumed it must have been a quote from the Bible. In any event, it had seeped so powerfully into my subconscious that, during my first year in St Kilda, I simply could not credit that some of my congregation, the unsolicited and unkempt street people who could not get their personal hygiene together, were true disciples of Christ. They did not look like—and certainly did not smell like—the serious and responsible Christian citizens that I mentally associated with authentic Christianity. My cultural spectacles were so strongly focussed on the model Christian, one who curiously and coincidentally looked like me, that no amount of evidence of warm faith emanating from a smelly street person convinced

121

me that this was a real Christian.

You can imagine my shock when I realised, with all the impact of a skydiver whose parachute had failed to open, that Jesus of Nazareth would have been an intensely smelly person. First-century Palestine was not blessed with abundant hot water; Jesus was an itinerant on the dusty road, without regular lodgings. If ever there was a street Messiah, it was him. Rapidly, I tried to adjust my cultural bearings to see with more biblical objectivity.

If twentieth-century hygiene was not a saint's stigma, what other marks had I got wrong? My inner agenda was utterly culture-bound. I aimed to change people to be like me. Whilst I had broadened considerably through exposure to other cultures overseas, I had never encountered the street culture before.

I had attended a private boys' secondary school and rubbed shoulders with a lot of sons of stockbrokers, lawyers, doctors and architects. I had gone through Monash law school with sons and daughters of stockbrokers, lawyers, doctors and architects. I had mixed with the same group, only on a much wider cultural palette, in Switzerland, but still they were articulate, tertiary-trained people. Poor people had been my legal clients as a lawyer, but I was firmly in control and my degrees hung intimidatingly on the wall behind me to remind them of my power and prestige.

It was not until my St Kilda days that it dawned on me

how totally contained life is. Indeed, you see reality from where you sit. Now, some of my friends within the congregation were not just poor but often dishevelled, on the nose and sometimes incoherent from psychotic episodes. But, paradoxically to me, they were still people of faith and hope.

Part of my self-discovery was how a middle-class background equips us to focus on the future. Much of life is organised around securing that future by working hard in school to get a good education and a well-paid job, and then working hard to save for a home deposit or for travel. Whatever the goal might be for middle-class people, it exists only in the future, and our culture disciplines us to sacrifice now in order to gain the future reward.

Street people, by contrast, are not futurists. They live almost entirely in the present. If they have money, instead of saving it, they throw a party, invite everyone, have a roaring good time and are impecunious again the next day. Living in the present is almost total. The really desperate live totally in the past and still try to settle deals for yesterday's debts and wrongs.

Now there is much to commend a futurist approach. It grants order and a planning that are great gifts, but the future goals are not necessarily morally superior to those of the present. Indeed, I could mount a solid biblical case that Jesus of Nazareth, who was accused of being a wine-bibber and party creature by his religious enemies, may well have thrown a party if he had any capital. He certainly had no house, or even the makings of a deposit, and he likened the dawning of God's new world to someone who would sell all and risk every asset for this kingdom—the celebratory festival of life.

Baggage Boy

Pat Mesiti

~

A classic example of needing the right kind of hearing occurred when I stepped off the plane at Sydney Airport after a fifty-two—that's right, fifty-two—hour flight. I hadn't shaved or showered and had only managed a couple of hours sleep. I felt tired and irritable and just wanted to ease into a nice hot bath with a good book and an urn of Italian coffee.

Ahead of me in the terminal was an immaculately dressed woman with more diamonds than a jewellery store. She turned to me and said, 'Yoo hoo, baggage boy.'

My response was less than pleasant. 'Lady, I'm not the baggage boy.'

Liz, my wife, stopped and chastised me. She looked at me like a Mobile Conviction Unit. I hate that.

'You're the one who talks about love and accepting people. If you'd listened properly you'd have seen she is asking for help.'

Don't you just hate it when they're right? I turned around with a mischievous look on my face and said, 'That'll be a buck a bag, lady.'

Had I listened properly I would have known that she was tired, alone and a little scared. I went back and gave her a hand.

What Would Jesus Do?

Tracey Stewart

~

One day Aaron, the son of golfer Payne Stewart, came home from school with several bracelets bearing the initials W.W.J.D., which stands for 'What Would Jesus Do?', the theme of Charles Sheldon's classic book *In His Steps*. In Sheldon's book, the question, 'What would Jesus do?' became the guiding principle that people chose to live by, regardless of the consequences. In recent years, the slogan 'What would Jesus do?' had become a resounding theme for many contemporary Christians as well.

As Aaron was showing Payne his bracelet, he said, 'Here, Dad. Why don't you wear one?'

'OK, I will,' Payne replied. 'Thanks, Aaron.' Payne put the bracelet around his wrist and fastened the clasp. He wore the bracelet everywhere, during golf tournaments, out for social occasions, wherever he went; he wasn't ashamed to be seen with the W.W.J.D. bracelet on his wrist.

Bobby Clampett, golf commentator for both CBS and

TBS television networks, was having breakfast with Payne at the Memorial Tournament in late May. A former PGA Tour player, whose Christian testimony on the Tour is highly regarded, Bobby noticed the W.W.J.D. bracelet Payne was wearing. 'Tell me the story behind the bracelet,' Bobby ventured.

Bobby recalls Payne's response. 'Payne told me the whole story—how Aaron had given him the W.W.J.D. bracelet and how it was sort of a silent witness to his faith. Then Payne turned to me, and looked at me as only Payne could do, and said, "How come you're not wearing one?" Payne had a way of saying things as a friend with a jabbing manner but always with a message behind it. I sat there, and I had absolutely no response to Payne's question. Finally, I stammered, "I . . . I . . . don't know." Basically what Payne was saying was, "Hey, I'm a public person, and I'm not afraid to talk about my faith in Christ, and I'm not afraid to wear it, and to let people know that it's a big part of my life, and you should too." I went home and I thought about that, and it kept gnawing at me. I said to myself, "I know I'm going to do this. I have to do this." '

Bobby put on a W.W.J.D. bracelet and has been wearing one ever since.

Cop This!

Grenville Kent

~

A Queensland Police Department envelope in your mailbox doesn't make your day. I felt $240 poorer as I opened it, remembering . . .

Darren was at work, so he asked me to pick up his car from his Gold Coast apartment. But his Control-a-Door kept jamming 20 centimetres up. I noticed where it was sticking, and banged it with my palm. It needed another hit from inside so I rolled under the door, trying to stay clean. I was in darkness, giving the door a bit more percussive maintenance when a female voice challenged, 'Are you right?'

'Yeah, I'm just borrowing Darren's car.'

'Who are you?' A no-nonsense voice. I saw young ankles and Doc Martens.

'I'm Grenville. Up from Sydney to talk at Darren's church, but this door's stuck, see?'

I pressed the button again, and the door rose perfectly.

129

It revealed a navy skirt, blue shirt, silver badges, young face, police cap. Gulp.

'Must've fixed it,' I mumbled like a guilty liar.

Then I noticed the car. A Commodore with the works: lumpy V8, low profiles, flared guards, spoiler. Every young car thief's dream.

'Um, he gave me his keys,' I said as she stared. 'Do you want to see some ID? Or phone him?'

'It's OK,' she smiled. 'I'm one of his flatmates. [Phew!] Let me guide you; it's a tight garage.'

We chatted above the bass burble of the mighty 350. I showed off my wife-and-baby snaps, and invited her to my meeting. Then I said goodbye and made my mistake—something I do every day in the shopping trolley I call a car. I put my foot down hard.

Before I knew it, the Commodore was sideways, then the other way, smoke pouring off the tyres, engine growling like a roused panther. I was gripped in the kidney-crushing racing seat, but my first panicked instinct was to hold tighter, including pushing my foot down flat.

My inner autopilot was opposite-locking furiously, and managed to drift the car straight through the gateway and point the right way down the street in a huge howlie that lasted at least 50 metres. Finally my wits caught up and my foot relaxed off the throttle.

I had broken the speed limit in first gear. I thought of

going back to apologise, but felt like The Big Prawn from Ballina, especially when I noticed her doubled over on the pavement laughing. So I kept going. Carefully. At the meeting I confessed to the audience that I'd done an accidental burn-out in front of the nicest cop in Queensland.

After that exhilarating power, I can't look at my car the same way. Or my life.

Jesus talked a lot about giving people power—to love, to live above problems, to grow, to achieve. Real religion is God under your bonnet—but it's never fanatical or out of control.

'God has not given us a spirit of fear, but of love and of power and of self-control' (2 Timothy 1:7). Inner power, used for love in a controlled way—and he's given us the keys!

Opening the envelope, I found a form: 'Dangerous Driving. Speeding. Disturbing the Peace. Arrest warrant awaits your next visit to Queensland.'

And on the other side a note: 'Ha, made you worry! I enjoyed your meeting (in plain clothes). Be safe. Regards, the Nicest Cop in Queensland.'

Penguins on Parade

Philip Yancey

~~

John Calvin urges us 'not to pass over, with ungrateful inattention or oblivion, those glorious perfections which God manifests in his creatures'. After several trips 'down under', I came away with a new reverence for 'those glorious perfections'.

On my first visit, I went whale-watching off the coast of New Zealand. Bobbing about in a rubber dinghy, we felt very small next to a sperm whale, whose tongue weighs as much as an elephant. The whale would rest on the surface for a while, then spout spectacularly a few times before plunging a mile deep to feed on squid.

Between whale sightings the guide, a Maori biologist, described other sea life. When a royal albatross soared by, he rhapsodised about these 'kings of the air'. Their wings, spanning 11 feet (3.3 metres), are so well-designed that an albatross can cover 600 miles with less flapping of its wings than a sparrow needs to cross a street. An albatross can sleep on the wing, flying on autopilot thanks to a small windspeed recorder in its bill that sends data to the brain, allowing it to make wing adjustments as the wind shifts. Also, an albatross has a built-in desalinisation factory. When it scoops up a mouthful of ocean, a series of tubes and membranes in the bill processes the water and extrudes excess salt.

I pressed the guide for more details. 'Countries in dry areas like the Middle East pay millions for desalinisation plants,' I said. 'Why can't we adapt the same technology on a larger scale?'

The Maori stared at me before responding. 'You're an American, aren't you?' he said at last.

On a subsequent trip last fall, I tried to experience wildlife with the eyes of worship, not of science. I spent three days on Australia's Phillip Island, a showcase of God's creation.

In the morning, as I jogged, kangaroos and wallabies thumped alongside. Cockatoos, all black except for brilliant yellow wing crescents, wheeled noisily overhead. I ran through eucalyptus forests with my neck craned upward, looking for the telltale puffs of gray that marked sleeping koalas. And at night, I watched the spectacle of shearwaters and fairy penguins.

A million short-tailed shearwaters return to Phillip Island on the same day each year, September 24. Each night they swoop toward shore in waves of hundreds and thousands, skimming the surface of the sea ('shearing the water') to pluck off tiny fish. Awkward birds, they tend to crash-land, take a few tumbles, and stagger indignant to their nests. They migrate 9000 miles from Alaska and the Aleutian Islands, farther than any other species. Most remarkable are their child-rearing habits. They fatten up their babies appropriately, but then one day the parents simply take off en masse, leaving the inexperienced nestlings to figure out how to fly, fish and navigate to Alaska on their own. Amazingly, almost half survive the ordeal.

For sheer entertainment, nothing compares to the nightly parade of the fairy penguins, who return to their nests after a day's fishing. At dusk they float shoreward in 'rafts' of ten or twenty. Less than a foot high, these midget penguins assemble along the beach in formation, waiting for courage to cross the expanse of sand. One feints, a few follow, then fear strikes and they all dash back into the sea. I watched one group make fifteen false starts before feeling brave enough to waddle across the sand. Lacking knees, they rock back and forth as they walk, holding their side-flippers out for balance.

C.S. Lewis suggests that observing God's creation is a holy calling:

For the beasts can't appreciate it and the angels are, I suppose, pure intelligences. They understand colours and tastes better then our greatest scientists; but have they retinas or palates? I fancy the 'beauties of nature' are a secret God has shared with us alone. That may be one of the reasons why we were made.

134

Flannery O'Connor once wrote an essay about her peacocks and the reactions they would get as they unfurled their feathers to present 'a galaxy of gazing, haloed suns'. One truck driver yelled, 'Get a load of that!' and braked to a halt. Most people would fall silent. Her favourite response came from an old black woman who simply cried, 'Amen! Amen!'

I think the Artist who designed the peacock rather enjoyed that response. It's certainly what I felt on Phillip Island.

Michael's Long Search

Philip Johnson

~

ichael Graham is something of a legend among spiritual seekers. He has rubbed shoulders with some of India's most spectacular gurus, and has also delved into the deepest aspects of human potential mind powers.

As a teenager he started to explore yoga and meditation. 'My father was a doctor,' he says. 'In fact he was one of Australia's first psychoanalysts. He was also something of a closet mystic. I began rummaging around in his library and found some books about the Indian spiritual traditions. I was fascinated by the promises held out in these disciplines for personal transformation.'

Not being one to do things by half-measures, Michael plunged headlong into what would become a thirty-year journey of rigorous exploration. He joined a yoga class in Melbourne and found the bodily exercises were easy. Yet, like many other adepts, he reached a cul-de-sac when he tried to meditate. Michael's teacher, who was from India, urged him to go there and meet a great guru who would guide him through these meditative barriers.

Like so many other restless youth, Michael left Australia in 1968 to pursue spiritual enlightenment. The guru Michael sought out was Swami Muktananda (1908–1982). 'I was Muktananda's first Australian disciple, amongst a handful of other Westerners. Today, Siddha Yoga is all around the world with more than 140 meditation centres and ashrams, and some 250,000 adepts.'

Back in 1968 Siddha Yoga was barely known inside India, let alone in the Western world. Siddha Yoga offers the initiate some dazzling charismatic or mystical experiences, which often occur in the presence or by the touch of the guru. 'I was seated on a tiger skin mat and Muktananda lightly touched me on the forehead,' Michael recounts. 'Nothing remarkable happened, and for several days afterwards I was still frustrated in my meditations.' Yet he soon had an explosive eruption of spiritual power within that was utterly mind-blowing.

'I was quietly meditating when there was the sudden powerful explosion inside me. I felt a charge of energy overwhelm me. I had instant insights, intuitions, perceptions and revelations. I had spontaneous bodily movements, called *kriyas*. I arose and was dancing around. I was laughing and crying at the same time, chanting and making utterances in other tongues. I was fully aware of what was happening around me, but I could not control this awakening. I ran outside, pole-vaulted a high fence. It was astonishing.'

Michael's experience became a legend in the movement, and Muktananda in his talks often referred to the Australian businessman whose experience was so powerful not even ten men could have held him down. After a few months of ashram life, Michael came back to Melbourne and organised Muktananda's 1970 tour of Australia.

Now, Michael was impressed with Muktananda as a powerful, charismatic man, but he never saw him as the embodiment of divinity. He was open to Muktananda's meditative methods but remained unsatisfied. So he began to cast around for supplements, while still remaining principally committed to Siddha Yoga. He became a guest in the apartment of Bhagwan Shree Rajneesh ten years before his international notoriety. He met other gurus such as H.W.L. Poonja and U.G. Krishnamurti.

In the 1970s he spent some time in America with Swami Rudrananda and Da Free John. He appreciated their insights but did not become their disciple. So like many others today, Michael tried to mix-and-match the very best elements of the Eastern spiritual traditions with the Western spiritual traditions. He was a friend of Francis Regardie, the great authority on the hermetic traditions, and also with Ingo Swann, the great American psychic who used his powers in the CIA's 'remote sensing' program.

'I read about 1500 books and experimented with the

human potential courses. I started out with Silva Mind Control and The Forum. All the while I maintained my commitment to Muktananda as my guru. I became the ashram manager in Melbourne, and then worked in Miami, Los Angeles and Ganeshpuri. After Muktananda died, a schism developed between the jointly nominated successors, Gurumayi and Nityananda. I saw at close hand the politics and antics of these two powerful, attractive people. I became Nityananda's international tour manager but eventually gave it up.'

Michael studied Harry Palmer's Avatar course and then became a licensed presenter of it in the US, France, New Zealand and Australia. He began designing his own program known as The Decision Principle®, and for a year led a group through the New Age-channelled book *A Course in Miracles*.

By the mid-1990s Michael's professional career began to slow down. 'I had spent nearly thirty years pursuing this pathway of enlightenment, and yet the promises remained unattainable.' At the back of his Melbourne home he built a self-contained flat and began spending time in complete meditative isolation.

One day, while settling into a chair, he had an extraordinary visionary experience. 'Within my chest cavity the figure of Christ appeared. I knew in an instant that it was he. This experience was wondrous beyond words. There was a warm welcome and a powerful sense that all would be right if I gave my life to him.' Yet Michael was uncertain what to do with this experience.

He left Melbourne and took up residence in California. 'My life soon reached a crisis where over a four day period my whole life caved in. The thousands of hours spent in meditation and chanting had added up to a big fat zero.' In his daily car trips he began surfing the radio dial and caught a few religious broadcasts. These shows reminded him of his mystical vision of Christ. 'Knowing of the importance of the power of decision, I wanted to give my life over to Jesus in a very public way. At that time Billy Graham was in town and so, before 22,000 people, I went forward and made my decision to follow.'

'A new journey for me has begun that starts and ends with grace,' Michael affirms. 'None of my other spiritual experiences can compare with the grace of the living Christ. My life is very different, and I live it each moment in gratitude. I have an inner peace and contentment that I never found through all the gurus and do-it-yourself experiences.'

The Day I Met the Wall With Hair

Pat Mesiti

I recall one time when I fell victim to prejudging people. It was the day I met the Wall With Hair.

The scene was in New Zealand. I was speaking in high schools and some Maori elders asked me to talk to a group of their people at their *marae* (their sacred ground).

Let me tell you something about these beautiful Maori people. When they sing it seems like heaven has turned up on earth. What voices! What harmonies! And they are so giving and loving, nothing is ever too hard for them. However, I didn't know this as I walked into the main building and immediately noticed half a dozen guys sitting in the back row. Actually, they weren't human. They were walls. They made Arnold Schwarzenneger look average. Not only were they huge, they were ugly. Each one had tattoos across his face like Spiderman, a nose wider than the Grand Canyon and lips that would make Mick Jagger jealous.

They sat with their arms folded and glared at me as I

started to speak. Something inside told me they were not Sunday school teachers. I later found out they were members of the fearsome Black Power motorbike gang.

As I talked I developed a mindset about these guys. They didn't like me, I decided. Their body language said aggressive, intolerant. And I wasn't sure that the topic for my presentation—'Purpose'—was all that relevant to them either.

The more I spoke the more annoyed I became because of my preconceptions.

I reached the end of my message—*phew!*—bowed my head and prayed. I prayed one prayer for them and another silent one for myself, something about surviving the meeting and making it home to my wife and daughters in one piece. Then I challenged the people who wanted a fresh start in life to come up to the front so that I could talk to them.

That was when I felt the earth move. I know New Zealand is right in an earthquake zone but this was a different tremor. This one had legs. I felt like I was in a scene from *Jurassic Park*. I noticed the glass of water on the podium moving with each rumble.

I looked up and there was the biggest and meanest part of the Wall With Hair bearing down on me. I had a sudden urge to hide under the furniture or run for the bathroom. He stopped and suddenly I was staring at his belly button. 'It's been nice knowing me,' I thought.

Then a funny thing happened. The belly button started

quivering as the surrounding stomach started heaving up and down. He was sobbing. Then that big, tough bikie bowed his head and mumbled, 'Sir, I want some o' dat.'

'Some of what?' I asked, stunned.

'Some o' dat what you talked about. Por-poise.'

'What?'

'Por-poise.'

Purpose, por-poise, I wasn't about to argue. When you're confronted by a seven-foot, 400-pound Maori, spelling isn't an issue. Life is—your own.

'I need help,' he continued as sobs melted into tears.

My heart turned to marshmallow and I tried to hug him, but my little arms only went halfway around his big waist. He wrapped his long tentacles around me and squeezed my face into his tummy. He cried, I cried, everybody cried. It was a special, tender moment as this person discovered he had something to live for and decided to pursue it.

We went back to his house and had fried bread and pork bones—a Maori delicacy—and he opened up and shared his life with me. He was the leader of a gang. They had committed some hideous crimes and most of his mates were in jail. Yet that night his life was changed. He found his 'por-poise'.

A while later I was back in a local school speaking to young people when, all of a sudden, the Wall With Hair showed up. Had the gang leader changed his mind? Had he decided to do me in for embarrassing him in front of his

143

mates? No. He asked me to go to the maximum security prison where his friends were and speak to them. Fortunately he was able to break through their preconceptions about this short funny Italian from Australia and they also opened up to me. The guys are still there, but I can tell you that on the inside they have become free.

The point I want to make is that at first I allowed tattoos, scars, broken teeth, unwashed hair, black leather jackets and body language to control my thoughts. When I put them aside, destiny was able to take over.

Kill the Dill with the Pill

Michael Frost

∾

I remember as a boy seeing a movie about the life of Christ. One scene in it had a profound impact on me—it haunted me for some time. It was a standard Hollywood treatment of Jesus' life and ministry (I think it was directed by Zefferelli and featured a galaxy of American movie stars) and, true to form, portrayed him as a vacant-eyed weirdo travelling about Palestine teaching about love and some strange Christ-consciousness.

But one scene knocked me off my feet. In this scene, Jesus and his disciples were playing some ancient game with a stone where they would throw the stone to each other, then pummel the person caught holding it too long. At school we used a ball and called the game kill-the-dill-with-the-pill. In the film, Jesus was the one caught with the rock and was the target of his friends. It was stacks on the mill as they all threw themselves on the hapless Jesus who lay prostrate on the ground.

As they climbed off him, to their horror, they found him motionless, his eyes closed, his face expressionless. A gasp of terror. We've killed him, they thought. Just as panic began to set in, Jesus flicked open his eyes and roared with laughter. It was a trick—and everyone enjoyed the joke. Everyone except me, watching at home on Saturday afternoon (probably around Eastertime when the networks always schedule these movies). It bothered me a great deal as I wrestled with the great theological dilemma as to whether or not Jesus would actually play tricks on his friends. As I said, it was a pretty daring scene in what was otherwise a typically conservative portrayal of the life of Jesus.

The primary source of my religious insight at this time came from the white leatherbound Bible my mother kept in the drawer of her bedside table. My mother had come from traditional working-class Irish Catholic stock and had been presented with the Bible at her first Holy Communion. It was filled with illustrated plates depicting scenes from various Bible stories: there was Daniel in the lions' den; Ruth and Naomi on the road to Palestine; Joseph and his coloured coat. And then there was, as the frontispiece, a commanding picture of Jesus, the good shepherd.

This picture of Jesus became almost my sole religious instructor. It depicted him as a gentle, caring, nurturing, loving shepherd. He had long, neatly parted ash-blond hair, curled carefully at his collar. His beard was clipped about his strong, square jaw and his eyes were piercing and icy blue. With one hand clasping his shepherd's crook, he reached with the other down to a stranded lamb, caught at the precipice.

The picture had convinced me that Jesus was earnest, decisive, competent—that he was as if on a quest with no time for the trivialities of life. He was reliable and dependable, but not quite human. He was an androgynous heavenly being who performed his missions of rescue and moved on to his next calling. Not unlike another hero of mine at the time, the Lone Ranger, whose well-known line, 'It looks like our work here is finished, Tonto', always signalled the end of another adventure.

So you can imagine why the idea of this immaculate cosmic shepherd playing kill-the-dill-with-the-pill disturbed me so much. It forced a radical reassessment that has been taking place to this day.

The Power of a Simple Invitation

Margaret Reeson

~

In the 1960s Alan Walker wanted to have a Central Methodist Mission congregation associated with the Lifeline building in Darlinghurst, an inner city suburb of Sydney. Twenty-four year old Noreen Towers was charged with this responsibility but she did not know how to do it.

A few weeks earlier, Noreen Towers had stood in the empty hall, looking at the lonely chairs and silent pulpit. In the quietness she prayed, 'Jesus, what would happen if you had my job? What would you do?'

A picture had begun to form in her mind, transforming the deserted space around her. She saw people, crowds of them, filling all the chairs, eager, passing in through the wide doors. Not only eighty people; the place was full!

She took a deep breath. It was true, that's what would happen. 'But Lord, how?'

That was weeks ago and she still didn't know the answer. Her friend Mrs Ames was setting up cups and saucers for morning tea after church and the pianist was turning pages in his hymn book while a handful began to arrive. It was hard to keep hold of the picture which had been so vivid. A crowded space? People pouring in through the front door? Maybe Jesus could do it, but it would have to be a miracle, and she was a very ordinary human being. In a few minutes it would be time for the morning service to start, and Noreen walked out to the steps leading outside into Flinders Street to look one last time up and down the street in case any other worshippers were coming.

And then she saw them. Two men sat in the gutter on the other side of the street. A thought came unprompted: 'Invite them to come in!'

Invite them? She looked again. They were sitting in the sun huddled into old coats, whiskery of chin, not very clean, and she could see the bottles poking out of their coat pockets. By the look of them, the bottles were probably half empty. Invite them? She hesitated. The men themselves had probably not even noticed the sign on the footpath, the open door of the church, nor the young woman standing in it. 'I don't suppose they'd like to come to church,' she thought. 'After all, no one else wants to!'

It seemed a ridiculous idea. How could she go up to total strangers like that and say, 'Come to church'? It was hard enough to knock on people's doors. But a couple of drunks in the gutter . . .

Afterwards it was hard to remember exactly how she had managed to cross the street, or what or who had propelled her. It was hard to guess, too, who was the more astonished, Noreen or the two men. The men saw a young woman suddenly appear in front of them, awkward and shy, waving towards the building across the road and saying, 'Would you like to come across to church?'

Noreen saw two startled faces, puzzled and staring at her in silence. Then one of them said, 'Well—er— lady, as a matter of fact we were just on our way there,' and looked as surprised to hear what he'd said as Noreen did.

She backed away, murmuring 'That's great . . .' and hurried back into the familiar space of the church hall.

The church service began, the singing thin with so few present. 'They won't really come,' Noreen thought as the little congregation bowed for the first prayers. 'They were just trying to get rid of me.'

Yet by the time she began to read the words from the Bible, there was the sound of movement at the back and she looked up to see the two men from the gutter sitting in the back row. They stayed through the service and at the end joined the congregation for cups of tea.

Noreen did her best to make them feel welcome. Their names, she learned, were Frank and Darryl. As they headed through the door, she asked, 'Will we see you next week?'

'Oh, yes, we'll be back next Sunday.' And they were gone.

150

'They won't be back,' her sensible, practical mind said. 'Once, maybe, but you mustn't get your hopes up.' 'They might be back,' her hopeful mind countered. 'We did our best to make them feel welcome—and they liked the hot cup of tea!'

By the following week, Noreen didn't know what to expect. Would Frank and Darryl come? During a prayer she heard a scuffle and when she looked up there they were. Not two men but six, all equally grimy and smelling of drink.

A week later, the six had become twelve and they filled up two rows at the back of church. Some of the established members were beginning to feel a bit anxious; an occasional drunk wandering into church was one thing, but two whole rows!

Over morning tea, Noreen asked one of the men, 'How did you know to come here to church this morning?'

'My mate here, he's a regular churchgoer here and he invited me along.' The mate had been once before.

The next week, there were eighteen men and Noreen was becoming very excited. A miracle seemed to be happening. But her enthusiasm turned to disappointment a week later. Only seven men arrived. 'It was too good to last,' she thought despondently.

'What happened to your mates?' she asked over morning tea.

'Lady, we nearly got caught, too. They have all been

charged with vagrancy and are guests of the government for the weekend!'

The picture in her mind was becoming clearer. A full church, yes, but not a church building filled with respectable, well-fed, comfortable people, but a church filled with people with great needs and a great sense of hopelessness. A place where a lonely person could find a friend, a rejected woman could find a welcome, a hungry man could have morning tea, a defeated person could find acceptance and new hope.

'If these men are so keen to come when their mate invites them, could there be others who'd come if I said hello in the streets or the parks and invited them, too?'

From so small and simple a beginning, a new thing began to grow.

The Kite Story

Gillian Dixon

~

October 1998 was the beginning of our son Andrew's illness. When he first became seriously sick we decided to pray. Jeremy set off up the hill of our rural property in Benloch, Victoria, as he usually did to walk and talk with the Lord. I stayed behind with the children to do the dishes.

While I was at the sink in the kitchen I looked out of the window to the hills and a clear picture came to my mind. The picture was like a slow motion movie of Andrew running along pulling a kite through the sky. He looked several years older than the little two-year-old lying ill in the room next to me. He had shorts on and was running and laughing, flying the kite. The only thing I couldn't understand about the picture was that his hair, in real life so white and fine, was thicker, darker, curlier.

Later that evening Andrew's health deteriorated quickly, so Jeremy and I drove him an hour-and-a-half to the Royal Children's Hospital in Melbourne. From the minute we walked in the front doors of Emergency and the first nurse saw Andrew, the enormity of the situation became clear. The medical staff knew only one thing that could give the particular symptoms that Andrew presented with, and that was leukaemia. Of the five things they looked for with leukaemia, Andrew had them all. A doctor explained they would take blood for testing. In an hour we would know.

Among the many things that happened in the ensuing hour, one was that I remembered the picture of the kite. I told Jeremy about it. Even if Andrew did have leukaemia, I wondered aloud, perhaps the picture meant God was with us and Andrew would live to fly a kite in a few years' time. However, I was disturbed because in the picture Andrew's hair had been so different.

The following five months were confusing and complicated. Although Andrew did appear to have leukaemia, his condition was so unusual that the doctors were unable to confirm it. And without a firm diagnosis, there could be no treatment plan other than bandaid therapy for each crisis as it arose.

Prior to Andrew becoming ill, we had felt God leading us to return to Perth, our original home, after twelve years away. With Andrew now constantly in a life-threatening position and the family living in Ronald McDonald House at the hospital, we felt it was important to push for Western Australia as quickly as possible. Apart from the fact our families lived there, there was a specialist in Perth we felt God wanted us to consult, Dr David Baker. There needed to be several major miracles for this to occur, and they happened. Andrew recovered sufficiently for us to leave the hospital for two weeks, during which we packed up our home and left town. An amazing aeroplane trip followed. I arrived in Perth carrying an extremely sick child attached to an oxygen pack strapped to my back and holding the tight little hand of another of our sons, five-year-old Benjamin.

Forty-eight hours after arriving in Perth, Andrew deteriorated again. I was due to drive to Princess Margaret Hospital to meet Dr Baker, so Jeremy's father gave me a car and directions to the hospital car park where I could leave it and walk via an underpass under the main road to the hospital's front door.

As I walked through the underpass carrying my sick baby, I suddenly noticed that all the walls were covered in beautiful mosaics. The design was kites, kites flying in the sky! When I came to the end of the underpass and walked up the stairs I couldn't believe what I saw. A big bronze kite was secured high on the side of the hospital building, and a long rope attached it to a bronze statue on the ground of a group of children flying it! Behind that on a wall was the Princess Margaret Hospital sign with its emblem—a kite flying high in the sky.

We were in the right place! God was with us! We soon discovered there were kites all over Princess Margaret Hospital; many months later we were still finding them.

Two weeks later Jeremy and our two older boys arrived in Perth by car. Then we received the definite diagnosis we had hoped never to hear: Andrew had juvenile myloid monocytic leukaemia, a rare form of leukaemia that required the severest of treatments, a bone marrow transplant.

Jeremy and I were taken to a meeting with several of the medical staff to discuss the treatment that Andrew would need to receive, the drugs involved and the side effects they would have in the short and long term. Eventually, through the waves of doom and disaster, I heard the words: '. . . and this will mean Andrew's hair will grow back darker and the texture will change.'

He was there before all time, the God of yesterday, today and forever. There is nothing he doesn't know, nothing that is hidden from him.

In September 2000, we went down to City Beach, the beach I grew up on, the place where we had a family picture taken before Andrew went into transplant twelve months earlier. We took with us a big colourful kite and Andrew flew it. He ran and he laughed, and his thick, curly, dark hair blew in the breeze.

Praying in the Spirit

Michael Frost

$\backsim$

Some years ago, I was preaching in a suburban church in Sydney. The worship leader had planned an open prayer time in the service, during which any member of the congregation may lead the others in prayer. Several people stood up and prayed out aloud, their prayers being met with resounding amens and *mm-mms* (deep evangelical grunt).

The last member of the congregation to pray was a cerebral palsied man named Paul. He was so physically disabled that his twisted, contorted mouth could not form words. He communicated with others by manipulating his quaking hand to point slowly to letters on a board attached to his wheelchair. Saliva ran fluently from the corner of his lips.

His prayer was one of the most moving I have heard. It began like this, 'Uuuurgh, mmmh, aaaaarh, uuuuurgh, uuuuurgh.' This bizarre groaning rolled on for several minutes. His deep inner thoughts were vented in that church for all to hear. No longer constrained by his twisted hand or his letter board, he gave voice to his full throated prayer.

To the untrained ear it might have sounded ugly. Some might have been uncomfortable at this long, gutteral moaning. But to the One to whom it was directed, it was music to his ears. I felt privileged to be an eavesdropper, to listen in on this magnificent prayer of faith. My love for Jesus was intensified as I heard the heartfelt yearnings of this contorted and disabled man. I didn't really need to deliver a sermon that day.

The 'Twenty-Third' Bush Ballad

Kel Richards

∽

(Psalm 23)

God is the Station Owner
And I am just one of the sheep.
He musters me down to the lucerne flats
And feeds me there all week.

When I'm feeling poorly
And at something less than my peak,
He leads me to the restfulness
Of a coolibah–shaded creek.

He teaches me not to break away,
Not to be a loner;
He teaches me to stick with his mob
And acknowledge him as my Owner.

Even when the droughts are bad
And I cross the Desert of Death,
God is close beside me,
So close I can feel his breath.

God is the one who holds the map
That gives me my direction,
And God is the one who guarantees
Provision for my protection.

Although there are dingos in the hills
And the paddocks are full of snakes,
God serves up a barbecue
Of beautiful T-bone steaks!

His patience and compassion
And forgiveness fail me never;
And I'll live with him in the Homestead
Beyond the end of forever.

Dean

Dave Andrews

~

Some of the most significant Christ figures in our lives may be ordinary, non-religious, even anti-religious, people who somehow—they may not even know how—at some moment represent something of the love of Christ to us. In my life there is a tough little Christ figure with thick glasses, spiky hair and empty gums, who goes by the name of Dean.

Dean started his life behind the eight ball. A little kid, at the mercy of big, merciless blokes, in an endless round of foster homes and special schools, Dean was knocked about a lot, and was constantly left feeling completely snookered. At the age of eighteen Dean was placed in a local hostel. I remember meeting him well, because at the time the only way Dean knew to express his emotions was by thumping people, and he was apparently so glad to make my acquaintance that he almost killed me.

Since that time Dean and I have become quite good mates. We share a passion for Rugby League Football, and are very passionate supporters of the Brisbane Broncos, whom Dean and I reckon are probably the best Rugby League team in the world. We regularly go out together with a bunch of friends, to have a barbecue in a park down by the Brisbane River, and Dean has even been known, now and again, to drag me into a game of what we call 'touch footy'—a very fast, and very skilful, non-contact training version of Rugby League—which is really far too fast and far too skilful for an old fella like me, but it's a lot of fun.

As time has gone by Dean has, thankfully, learned to express his love for his friends much more tenderly than he used to. Dean is now known more for his trademark quick chuckle, cheeky smile and kindly touch than for thumping people.

Not long ago, a brother-in-law of mine sadly lapsed into an episode of psychotic despair, jumped off the Storey Bridge which spans the Brisbane River, and tragically killed himself. Needless to say, I was devastated. When I told everybody at church how devastated I was, I noticed Dean, standing in the back of the room, listening intently to me. Before I realised it, he made his way to the front, where I was standing, and stood beside me, with his arm around me, quietly waiting until I had finished what I was saying. Then, all of a sudden, he embraced me, gave me a huge hug, and said, 'Don't worry Dave. I'll be your brother-in-law.' I'll never forget that simple, unpretentious gesture of care. At that moment Dean represented the love of Christ to me.

Taking Up the Cross— 21st Century Style

Barry Chant

～

Large crowds were following Jesus. So he turned to his disciples and said, 'Make the people sit down.' There was much grass in the place and the people sat down. There were about five thousand men, plus women and children.

Then Jesus called the chief musician to direct the singers and other players. They played loudly on harps, lyres, timbrels and flutes. And the people stood to their feet and sang psalms many times over. They clapped their hands and made a joyful noise to the Lord.

Then Jesus said:

'If anyone come after me and does not love his father and mother, his wife and children, his brothers and sisters—yes, even his own life—he cannot be my disciple.

'And if he does not put on rich garments and the finest raiment and believe that he shall have whatever he says, he cannot be my disciple.

163

'For he who follows me shall have rings on his fingers and bells on his toes and he shall have music wherever he goes.

'For he who follows me must have a good self-image and see himself as worthy of the kingdom of God.

'In the same way, any of you who wants to be my disciple must realise that by following me, he will have the best of everything. He will certainly ride in the latest model chariot and have all the denarii he needs. He will be dressed in fine linen and live in sumptuous palaces.

'Indeed, whatever he desires he shall have, just as whatever I desire, I have.

'Do not worry about providing for your family or future. Just name it and claim it, confess it and possess it, blab it and grab it, believe it and receive it and all will be yours. For God wants you to be healthy, wealthy and wise.

'You have a unique destiny. You must fulfil your potential. Only believe.'

And the people rejoiced to hear his words, for he spoke as one having much wealth and prosperity, and they longed to go and be likewise.

And Jesus continued to teach them, saying,

'Anyone who follows me must lay down his cross and go before me. For suffering is the result of sin and my way is a sinless way.

'Blessed are you when all men speak well of you, when they praise you and support you, for so they have always

164

spoken of the prophets of God. Therefore, if any man come after me, let him take out his wallet, get all that he can, and follow me.'

And again the people wondered at the gracious words that proceeded from his mouth, for they sounded too good to be true.

Then the musicians began to play a sweet maskil of a daughter of Israel, saying, 'Sacrifice and offering you did not desire, for the gospel is free, but as it is written in the volume of the book, "Just as I am, I come to Thee." '

And Jesus said to His disciples, 'Tell the people to close their eyes and bow their heads.' And the people did so.

And Jesus said, 'If you would like to make a decision to give your heart to me, I beseech you to raise your right hand. Fear not, for no one can see you.'

There were some who were afraid, but at the words of Jesus, they raised their hands.

Then Jesus said, 'I see that hand. Is there another?' And it came to pass that when all the people had responded, Jesus asked them to stand to their feet, and behold, there were some who did stand.

Then Jesus said, 'While the music is playing softly and the choir is singing, this is my commandment that you step out here to the front, so I can pray for you.'

And as some of the people hesitated, he continued to instruct them, saying, 'Do not be afraid. I will not keep you long. Only the heathen think they will be heard for their empty repetitions. The prayer will be brief and there are some disciples here who will talk to you for a few minutes and give you a little scroll. Your friends will wait for you. You will be home in time for dinner.'

And lo, some of the people did come, and they took the little scroll.

But he did not tell them that it would be sweet as honey in their mouths but turn their stomachs sour (Revelation 10:9).

And he did not tell them that to follow him they would indeed carry his cross.

And he did not tell them that it was only by losing their lives that they would find them.

So they went away happy.

For a while.

The Coober Pedy Cup

Kerry Medway

~

The long weekend in October is the highlight of the opal-field calendar. Thousands of visitors from surrounding sheep and cattle stations, old Cooberpedians from Adelaide and members of the racing fraternity arrive by car, aeroplane and horseback in a flurry of dust, sweat and flies.

Members of Parliament, graziers and socialites mingle with open-shirted miners and jackaroos, all in their R.M. Williams boots and hats. It is Cup Weekend, a time for yarning, boozing, betting and meeting old friends, when the ritual of 'cracking a stubbie' (opening a cold can of beer) is followed more closely than the form of the horses themselves.

On the Saturday, miners bid for ownership of a racehorse for the weekend. Hundreds of dollars are outlaid for a wild bush brumby from a nearby cattle station, each miner longing for a 'Gunsynd' winner rather than a 'Radish' loser, and the glory of a silver-plated trophy on the wall of his dugout.

One year, just before the running of the Coober Pedy

Cup, tragedy struck. The race-caller disappeared, rumour having it that he had developed laryngitis but, if the truth was really known, having over-indulged at the bar. The organisers were presented with a major dilemma. How could they run the main event without a dramatic description over the public address system? Someone, whom I'm sure lived to regret it, suggested the local preacher to call the race. Before I knew where I was, six big burly 'racing officials' had persuaded me to take over, leading me firmly towards the saddling enclosure to examine the horses and their jockeys. No amount of protesting would convince them that I knew little about horses and absolutely nothing about calling a horse-race.

With a racing guide in my hand, I frantically studied the horses and the jockeys, looking for a three-legged horse or any other peculiarities which I might readily identify.

As I mounted the race-caller's stand, I silently sent a prayer to heaven, thanking the Almighty that there were only six horses in the race. I stood high above the crowd, microphone firmly grasped in my hand, putting on my best 'Des Hoystead' voice and steeling myself for the big event.

The horses were on the track. The spectators abandoned the bar and lined the fence for the main event, the running of the Coober Pedy Cup. The excitement of the crowd gave me fresh confidence and I delivered the most dramatic pre-race build-up I could muster.

After two false starts, the horses were off in typical fine

bush fashion, leaving a trail of dust behind their galloping hooves. The leading horse quickly broke away from the others, spreading the field behind him. I began my commentary in style. It was easy to identify the horses along the back straight, as they rode in single line towards the home turn. Being a race-caller had to be a cinch.

Then, as the horses turned towards the finishing line, disaster struck. I discovered that as the horses were running towards me the jockeys crouching behind the horses' heads with only their white helmets in view, I couldn't tell one from the other. I stood with my hand frozen to the microphone, unable to utter a word. Then, drawing on all my preaching skills, I began to call the most dramatic finish ever to be heard in a Coober Pedy Cup, making up the race-call as I went along, without a clue as to which horse was winning the race. I knew which horse was leading on the back straight and hoped against hope he was still in front at the end of the final turn.

As the horses crossed the finishing line, my voice cracked and a shiver of horror shot down my spine as I realised my dramatic race-call was all wrong. The horse I had so skilfully described as the winner was not even amongst the first three place-getters!

There was an agonising pause as I watched the crowd below me tear up their betting slips in disgust. Then, as they realised the true identity of the winning horse, their disgust turned to anger as they feverishly searched through the dust for their winning tickets. I quietly longed for a giant willy-willy to whisk me away from the angry and confused mob to my peaceful home under the ground.

Such was not to be. I meekly descended the stairs and quickly melted into the crowd, vowing never again to call a race, let alone the premier event of the Coober Pedy racing calendar.

The Crazy Hitchhiker's Guide to Reality

Ruth Pollard

~

Most of us have split our sides laughing at the tormented antics of the dysfunctional characters played by the comedian Woody Allen. With Woody Allen, art imitates life because he takes his own psychiatric difficulties and portrays them in his movies. He creates humour out of his own real depression.

My life story is a lot like those Woody Allen movies. And depending on which way you look at it, it could either be a huge tragedy or a huge comedy.

It all began in the halcyon days of the '60s, when drugs, rebellion, free love, rock music and alternate lifestyles reigned supreme. But—wouldn't you know it?—I was born into one of the most rigid Christian sects. Whatever the free-loving '60s people were into, I was prohibited from sampling because God forbade it all.

It's one of life's ironies that I was born into this sect,

because regimented patterns of black and white thinking describes me to a tee.

I was born with an obsessive-compulsive disorder (OCD). That means I can't help but be scrupulous about the way I handle life. If you saw Jack Nicholson in *As Good As It Gets*, you'll know a bit about what OCD people endure. My life is consumed with endless obsessions, ruminations and rituals.

My husband cheekily says I like to complicate things with more imaginary and exaggerated situations than Basil Fawlty!

I can't leave the house without first repeatedly checking to see that both the iron and stove are off and all the windows and doors are locked. If I've used a tea towel once it must go immediately into the wash. If I find a freckle I obsess that I have inoperable cancer and run off to five different doctors to get a verdict. I can't stop at one because it is the nature of the disorder to doubt whatever I'm told. Maybe the first doctor did not check thoroughly. Maybe the pathology results were swapped with someone else's. And so it goes on.

I not only make life awkward for my husband and myself, but I involve everybody in my madness. It's like a game of Snakes and Ladders. Before I was married I would occasionally take my mother on holidays, and prior to leaving I would, of course, do the rounds to check on the windows and doors. We would drive to the top of the street and I would have to return to check them once more. I would drive a bit further along the road only to turn back and check again. It's amazing that we ever made it to our destination. Of course, as soon as we arrived I would head for the nearest phone and ask my neighbour to check the windows and doors. This became such a predictable pattern that my neighbour used to anticipate my phone calls.

I once even brought the railways to a halt. On a trip home from work, I noticed through the window what looked to me like a baby wrapped in blankets on the side of the tracks. I was so sure the baby was there that I ruminated about it all the way home. Overtaken by this anxiety attack, I raced into the house, grabbed the phone and alerted the railway staff to investigate. Pity the poor staff finding their way along the tunnels to check. Needless to say it was just a bundle of cloth—definitely no baby.

It wasn't until I was thirty-five years of age that I discovered I had OCD. Abnormality was the norm. Nobody close to me was normal either; and with everyone so much like Woody Allen characters, how could I know what was normal?

My most manic obsessions have all been to do with faith. As I disbelieve a lot, I could have been the gospel character 'doubting Thomas'. The sect I grew up in unwittingly nurtured within me an utter fear of God. My greatest anxieties and doubts were that I was unforgiven and beyond the pale. I can laugh about it now, but at the time all my worries about God, faith and forgiveness were horrible nightmares.

There were times when I expressed some of my fears or doubts to other Christians. I am grateful that there were those who listened and were very supportive, and the times they set aside to help surely relieved the pressures a bit. My principal supporter and friend was my sister Valerie, without whom I would not be where I am today.

Sadly not everyone was helpful. Some said that all my troubles were caused by demons. All kinds of remedies for dealing with them were prescribed, but I was no better. Others attributed my problem to a lack of faith. So like a spinning wheel going nowhere, I would throw all my mental and spiritual energy into working up feelings of faith and belief. I would spend enormous amounts of time praying and reading the Bible, and accosting people to tell them they should repent. Yet all the while I was afraid of God. No matter what I did, my spiritual life too was just like that game of Snakes and Ladders.

Now the incredible thing is, I did survive all this madness and chaos. God uses people and situations to heal and empower us. This is what happened to me.

My discovery that I had OCD came about through meeting the man who is now my husband. He had read about the condition before we met and, watching my behaviour, suggested that I had it. At the time I was virtually crippled in my daily living by anxieties and obsessions. I was referred to a psychiatrist, who was amazed that I had managed to get so far—even completing a law degree—with such a complex set of obsessions.

174

OCD is caused by a deficiency in a brain chemical called serotonin, and there are certain drugs that can be prescribed to help restore at least partial balance. The first drug I was put on did start lowering the panic attacks, but, in classic Woody Allen style, a smooth ride was out of the question. Out of the thousands of people who take this drug, I had to have the most extreme side effects: lethargy, nausea, depression, facial migraine, dryness of the mouth, extraordinary weight-gain, involuntary teeth grinding, and arthritis-like symptoms in my ankles and feet. The cure was almost as bad as the disease! After a lot of trial and error, I finally found a tablet that, if taken in continuous minute dosages, helps me feel better without a lot of the crippling side effects.

By the time my disorder was diagnosed, I had long since left the sect of my childhood. During all the years I belonged to it I never understood the empowering forgiveness that Jesus gives us. I struggled to grasp God's love for me. Amazingly, when I was in my mid-twenties I did take a step of faith to embrace that love, and that was an important moment in my journey. Yet it took ten more years to find out I had a mental illness problem.

All the well-meaning Christian people around me did not understand my problem. The most upsetting thing to happen was when a Christian friend told me that God had shown her my problems were attributable to a lack of faith. I felt incredibly disappointed. I believed that, because she was so holy,

God did speak to her. But somehow I knew that if Jesus were here face-to-face with me, he would not have said that. He would know what I was going through. If God had *truly* spoken, surely the message would have been: 'Go to a doctor, you're ill.'

So where am I now? Since treatment began six years ago, I have found out a lot of things about myself and about God. Much of what I thought about God was so skewed. I have had to re-evaluate the basis of my faith and my impressions of God, as well as come to terms with living through a mental illness. On the one hand, I have had to accept my limitations and come to grips with reality. I have had to learn to restrain my scrupulosity, which is no mean feat (there is no simple formula). On the other hand, I have found that, yes, there are some historical and legal facts that show it makes good sense to trust the gospel records about Jesus. I have also had to learn to expand my horizons about who God is and how he treats us.

All this has meant dismantling and discarding an awful lot of junk that I picked up on the way. I have had to 'spring clean' my mind. My ritual habits of checking and worrying have not vanished, but they are now contained. A lot of this is due to my treatment and the way my husband has helped me to grow and cope. Ultimately it is the work of God's Spirit in me.

This is the funniest thing of all: God invites us to trust, and by trusting we find the liberty to live and grow and become the person we are meant to be. All of my life has been consumed with going off in the opposite direction through doubt, fear and trying to be a control freak. But I have come to realise that God invented humour, and the most laughable thing has been my unwillingness to let God help me.

All the while I was asking for a whiz-bang miracle, but God was offering me a different kind of lifeline. I was busy being manic and doing kooky things, but God was quietly asking me to stop, calm down, listen and accept I had a mental health problem. I was looking at it solely as a spiritual problem, but God wanted me to find healing.

Part of the Answer

Gordon Moyes

When I was a boy growing up in Box Hill, I did not have the faintest idea that I would ever go into the ministry. My family had no connection with the church, my parents never attended during my father's life and after his death my mother supported us while we went to Sunday school as children, but never attended herself.

The slender line of contact with the Sunday school was the only continuing contact that the church had with me until the time when I was thirteen and I met a new girl with blonde hair who came to our church, by the name of Beverley, and fell head over heels in love with her. As she and her mother asked me questions about the Christian Endeavour, I determined that I would join as well. So I became an active member.

After my commitment to Christ and baptism, I became a member of the church but I still had no thought of entering the ministry. I was having too much fun.

High school days were some of the happiest days I could possibly imagine. I took no part in any Christian group at high school; I was far too mischievous, causing too much disruption with teachers and other pupils, loved sport, musicals and, in particular, athletics far too much for the meetings, discussion, Bible study and prayer of the Christian groups.

The turning point came when I was seventeen. At a Christian Endeavour meeting two rather nondescript students from the Churches of Christ theological College of the Bible came and spoke to us about what life was like as a theological student. For the first time I realised that people who trained for the ministry were just very ordinary people like myself.

Sometime in the fifth year of high school, I was going through a period of intense inner rebellion against the school and many of the influences in society at large. My mate, Ziggy, and I discussed the merits of Marxism, socialism, the degeneracy of capitalism and democracy, and the plight of the poor within society. At the same time, I was rebellious against authority and was doing all I could to disrupt the course of events at school.

Someone, somewhere, at some time, said a sentence bluntly that turned my life around. I will never forget the sentence although I cannot remember who it was that faced me with it. Pointing out the consequences of my disruptive behaviour and radical attitudes that person said, 'In this life you are either part of the problem or part of the answer. Which are you?'

I pondered that question as I became increasingly more involved in trouble. I decided then and there that I was going to be part of the answer to society's problems rather than part of the problem. I determined to help other young people and threw myself immediately into running all kinds of youth programs, organising and compering city-wide youth concerts that attracted hundreds of young people on the first Saturday of each month, and began taking an active leadership role in church youth camps. I wanted to get alongside troublesome mischief-makers in the community—young delinquents and breakers of the law in whose number I had been so recently prominent.

In my seventeenth year, I decided that there could be no other task in my life than to be a minister of the gospel of Jesus Christ.

I told other people joyfully. I was invited immediately to be a temporary preacher at a little inner suburban church at Newmarket and I took my first services when I was seventeen years of age. I preached with conviction, urging people to commit their lives to Jesus Christ. I brought my friends to services. It was not a big church, and in my first service there were only fourteen people present and eleven of them were my friends or relatives. But I was going to be a preacher of the gospel.

My commitment to Christ and to ministry was confirmed by a number of people. One of my teachers started talking to me seriously during a spare period at three o'clock one afternoon and kept talking to me until 6.00 p.m., trying to convince me not to become a minister. He urged me, instead, to get into the infant television industry that would soon arrive in Australia, or to go to acting school and go on the stage, or to enrol in teacher's college and help young people by being a teacher—in fact, anything and everything that may fulfil my particular interests and talents other than the ministry.

At 6.00 p.m. the cleaners wanted to lock the door of the classroom, so finally he said to me, 'I am a practising Christian. I am absolutely thrilled you are going into the ministry, but I wanted to make sure that the conversion that has occurred in your life was for real. I believe you should go into the ministry only if you have no other possible alternative. I have offered you every conceivable alternative, but you keep insisting on answering Christ's call and going into the ministry. Well, you go with my prayers and my blessing.' Unknown to me, for the three hours he had been praying that I would become a minister, but was determined that he would keep out of the ministry any person unless they had a depth and reality of call.

From the moment of my decision to enter the College of the Bible, I began work, practising preaching on upturned banana boxes in my lounge room at home and taking as many services, youth camps and youth activities as I could. At the beginning of the next year I packed my bags, left home and commenced studying theology at Melbourne University. An entire new chapter of my life was opening up.

Who would ever have thought that one of the young mischief-makers of Box Hill would, in later years, come back to conduct evangelistic missions in the town hall?

The Childbirth Conspiracy

Angela Eynaud

~

When I gave birth to my first child, the whole race of women was cast in a new light. Perched on my donut cushion and bleary-eyed from lack of sleep, I watched other new mothers walking the corridors of the maternity hospital in varying states of discomfort, weariness and anxiety. They too had passed through the fiery furnace of childbirth.

I know it was probably the after-effect of too much pethidine, but other women had suddenly become my sisters and we were linked together by our shared experience.

It was a difficult and complicated birth and my first encounter with intense pain. The cosy, safe parameters of my life had been breached. I was experiencing both shock at what I had gone through and the exhilaration of becoming a parent. I guess that's what is unique about childbirth—two of life's great challenges at the same time.

It was as if I had discovered a secret. I'd found what really mattered. I'd been stretched to the limit of what I could bear and returned forever changed.

During antenatal classes we'd been told some amusing stories of women who in the middle of their pain had struck out at their partners or sworn at them, cursing them for having 'got me into this'. The cry that burst from me was 'What was God thinking of?'

When my little sister arrived for a visit, my heart swelled to embrace all those who I suddenly realised were genetically predestined for the same soul-searing torture. It was not an experience I'd wish on my worst enemy, and here was my little sister ignorant of the trick played on her by her own body. I wanted to grab her and impress on her, 'Never have a baby. It's all a dreadful conspiracy. They don't tell us what it's like so that we'll go on producing. No one who knows would willingly submit to it!'

So why did I go back and do it all again three years later? Because I was right. I had discovered a secret. I had been changed by my suffering, and my experience of being a mother would change me even more.

The tiny life I had brought into the world became, over the next weeks and months, so intricately bound with my own that it seemed in some ways never to have been severed from me at all. The rewards of motherhood so outweighed the costs that I became a convert to the cliché I'd been raised on: 'It's all worth it in the end.'

Some years after becoming a mother for the second time I met Ruth. As a complication of a pre-existing eye defect, this brave woman gradually lost her sight during pregnancy. By the time she gave birth she was completely blind.

One day she was asked whether she'd ever explored possible cures for her sight loss. She answered, 'No, not at this stage. I reconciled myself to sight loss during pregnancy as the cost I had to pay. My experience of motherhood has been so wonderful that I don't feel the least bit shortchanged.'

Birth presents us with a parable worked out in our own bodies—that the foundational experience of parenthood is the experience of selflessness. The cost to the mother in giving the gift of life is extraordinary, but the blessing is so great that it renders the sacrifice insignificant in hindsight.

It is a lesson well-learned, for the ongoing experience of parenthood will require of me the same self-sacrifice in different forms over and over again.

The Problem of Pain

Phillip Jensen

∼

'Therefore pride is their necklace; they clothe themselves with violence.' Psalm 73:6

'I think that suffering makes belief in God impossible,' the atheist thundered at me.

I paused to work out what to say next. And in the pause a small voice came from one of the corners of the room. 'I was a prisoner of war, when I was young. I saw a lot of suffering in the camps.'

It was the middle of a dialogue meeting. The hosts had done marvellously in bringing together a group of non-Christians who were willing to discuss Christianity.

The atheist took the first hour of the meeting with all the usual objections to Christianity. Finally he had reached the problem of suffering as if he were the first one to have ever thought of it and as if Jesus did not know anything about it.

However, it was the intrusion of the quiet woman in the corner that brought a standstill to the debate that had been raging. It is hard to know what to say to somebody who starts talking of the horrors of their youth. The whole nature of the conversation changes when we are not talking about the suffering of the world but entering into the reality of suffering of another person.

I turned the conversation to her, conscious that the intellectual weight of the atheist was about to be joined by the emotional and personal weight of the ex-prisoner of war.

'I saw brutal things done to people. I watched all my family suffer. I suffered a lot of things myself.'

Sometimes in talking with people, different languages are used. In the dialogue meeting up until this point we had been using the language of logic, argumentation, polemics. When this lady started talking so personally of her suffering, it became insensitive and impossible to continue in that language. Her revelation required the language of sympathy, empathy, personal relationship.

The atheist did not understand the change in language. 'Suffering, that is what tells against God. Tell him about it: you do not find believers in prisoner-of-war camps, do you?' His insensitivity appalled me.

'It must have been a terrible time,' I reflected.

'No, that's not what I want to say,' she rebuked me. 'I do not want your sympathy. I want to tell you of what that suffering taught me about God!

'I just want this man here,' she said, pointing to the atheist,

187

'to understand what suffering does to you. It did not bring me to atheism but to God. For when you are absolutely helpless like that there is no one else to turn to. I would be just like you, proud and full of my own competence, except I had to live for those years seeing the horrors of evil, and depending on God for survival.

'People did not give up on God in the camps—many of us found him there.'

The Call of God

Fred Nile

~

September 1955 was the month when I heard the call of God to give my life completely to him for his service. Not long after announcing our engagement, Elaine and I went as part of a 300-strong New South Wales delegation to the National Christian Endeavour Convention in Brisbane. The theme of the convention, written in giant letters across the front of the Brisbane City Hall, was 'This Decisive Hour'.

It was a wonderful ten days. Each morning we shared in Bible studies and discussion groups. In the afternoons we went on outings and country tours in fleets of buses. Each night brought a crowded, enthusiastic rally in the City Hall, with a 200-voice choir, musical items and a powerful message from the guest speaker, the Reverend John Ridley of Sydney. He was the evangelist who challenged Arthur Stace, who later became famous for writing the word 'Eternity' on the streets of Sydney.

189

He challenged me, too. Night after night, the theme 'This Decisive Hour' hit me between the eyes until I understood God was speaking to me personally. This was *my* decisive hour—the decisive hour for the rest of my life. On the final night, God's presence was so real my body began to tremble. I knew he was calling me.

But what was it he wanted me to do? I tried to reason with him. If it was something I'd *like* to do then I would say yes. But he would not answer my questions. It seemed the call was completely open-ended. God was saying: 'Will you give your whole life to serve me with no restrictions, no reservations, a blank cheque?' I suddenly had an alarming thought. It might be something so terrible that, if I knew what it was, I would say no!

Finally I assumed God was asking me if I was willing to die in his service. 'Lord,' I said, 'deep down I would rather live for Christ than die for Christ. But if you want me to die for you, perhaps on some lonely mission field, then I am completely willing.'

I had not the slightest inkling of the surprising places that prayer would lead me over the years to come.

190

The Platypus

Ross Clifford and Philip Johnson

❧

At the close of the eighteenth century, European zoologists dismissed out of hand reports about a creature that was described as possessing the following characteristics: it was a furry, rabbit-sized, webbed-footed mammal, had a duck-bill, a reproductive system like a reptile, lived in rivers and laid eggs. In the mind set of the day such a creature was an impossibility—it was out of their frame of reference and contradicted all prior experience and knowledge. Then in 1884 a female of the species was shot after having laid an egg. The astonishing reports could now be verified. The prevailing obstinacy in disregarding the creature could no longer be honestly sustained without deliberately ignoring the evidence. The creature was the platypus and these days can be seen in various zoos.

The platypus reminds us of the resurrection: many refuse to accept it because it doesn't fit in with their presuppositions, even though there is strong evidence on its behalf.

The Ironman

Michael Frost

~

Once on the TV program *Wide World of Sports* I saw the Ironman contest telecast from Hawaii. This is a quite remarkable event. Each contestant must complete three legs of what is surely the most gruelling race on earth. The first section is a 3.8 kilometre swim. That's about seventy-five laps of an Olympic-size pool—you could count me out in the first leg! Then, the participants must ride a bicycle for a mere 180 kilometres. That's roughly the distance from Sydney to Newcastle, a trip I regularly make and still complain about when it takes around two hours—in a car. And finally, they must run for forty-two kilometres to the finish line.

Now, it's not as though they have all the time in the world to complete these legs. There are time limits on all three sections, so if you don't make each one, you're out of the race.

Watching this on TV, I saw someone I must tell you about. He is in his late forties/early fifties, with a son in his late teens/early twenties. His son is severely physically disabled with cerebral palsy and is unable to walk. What this man did was to complete the Ironman competition in Hawaii by *carrying* his son all the way around the course.

For the swim leg, he put his boy in a rubber dingy of sorts and, harnessing himself to the dingy, dragged him the whole 3.8 kilometres. For the bike ride, he had a bicycle custom-built with a large seat in front for his son. And for the run, he pushed his boy in what looked like a big pram all the way to the finish line.

The remarkable thing is that he just made each leg under the allotted time. And this got many of the officials thinking. If he could complete the course under time with his adult son in tow, what could he do on his own? When asked this, the man responded by saying, 'Alone? What would be the point?' For him, completing the course wasn't any great achievement, but completing it with his *son* was worth all the agony. It's a deeply moving true story of a man who models what God is like.

God can complete the race quite easily without us. He can exhibit mastery and control. He's a winner. But for him there would be no point in doing it alone. He wants to complete it with us in tow.

As St Augustine once said, 'Without him, we cannot; without us, he will not.'

Love Spelled Y-O-U

Glenn Williams

~

It was Saturday night and I arrived home late in the evening after having to spend the day at work. My wife was in bed, as were the children. I went into my daughter's bedroom to kiss her goodnight, when I saw a note lying on the floor.

I picked it up and began to read it in the dim light. As I read it, my eyes filled with tears.

Dear Dad,

It seems like such a long time since we talked about things. The other day I woke up just a little bit late and raced to your bedroom to tell you that I loved you, but you had already left for work. The disappointment on my face must have shown, as Mum gave me a big cuddle and offered to drive me to school. She reassured me that I could tell you tonight when you got home.

I didn't have a good day at school. Tracy has a new friend today, so she didn't want to have lunch with me. Jackie was away sick. So I didn't have a friend to sit next to in class. The disappointment on my face must have shown, as the teacher sat down next to me and told me how good my work was.

Finally, school was finished. I was so looking forward to you coming home from work that I even made a special card for you. I put lots of kisses and hugs inside, and put it on the dinner table next to your plate.

I ran to pick up the telephone when it rang, and was excited when I heard your voice. But you were busy and didn't have time to talk, and quickly asked me to get Mum. Mum came back to the kitchen where I was helping her get dinner ready and told me that you were going to be getting home a little bit later than usual and wouldn't be having dinner with us. The disappointment on my face must have shown, as Mum said that you would wake me up when you came home. I left the card on the table so you could see it when you got home.

When I woke up the next morning, you had already left. I was very sad. I went into the kitchen to have breakfast and saw that you had not opened the card I prepared for you. Mum came into the kitchen. The disappointment on my face must have shown, as tears began to run down my cheeks. I asked Mum why you had to go to work today since it was Saturday, and you'd said we could go shopping together. Mum replied that work was very busy at the moment, and it was important for you to go to work so you could earn enough money for us to be happy.

The disappointment on my face must have shown, as mum gave me a cuddle and told me that you loved me. I know that. But it would have been more special hearing it from you.
Love, Emma.

How did you feel when you read this story? It seems that we live in a culture that is constantly striving for material security, only to miss out on providing the real security our kids need to have—love that is real. Love that means being there for your family during the growing years.

It has become too easy to justify our absence from home because we have convinced ourselves that financial security can be obtained by working longer hours. We justify spending less time with our families by claiming that the time we do spend with them is 'quality' time. We become experts at making such excuses and have substituted *words* of love and affirmation for practical demonstration.

This next week, why don't you take some time to sit down with your spouse and re-evaluate your priorities and values in the light of what your family needs most—YOU!

Shopping for Jeans

Chad Armstrong

～

I went shopping the other day and discovered a new spiritual gifting—one I hadn't really noticed before. And I certainly hadn't noticed how proficient I'd become in it without even trying.

I'm talking about the spiritual gift of 'shopping'.

I was looking for jeans. I'd grown out of an old pair and was looking to replace them. Then it came over me. The choices of jeans! Did I want blue, dark blue, black or maybe linen ones? Or maybe a new pair of 'cargos'? What about 'chinos'? Flat-fronted? Drawstring ties, buttons or zipper? Long? Baggy? This was a serious decision to be making. The wrong choice could mean the total ruin of my fragile self-image.

Choices. And so I did what any self-respecting capitalist would do. I searched for the best bargain. Myer, Just Jeans, JeansWest, David Jones, Jag, Calvin Klein, General Pants Co., Country Road, Colorado, Esprit Men. I was like a wild man hunting a defenceless prey. In my hands was a sturdy weapon, my Visa.

I was on a mission for the best fitting, best priced, best looking, most practical pair of pants. Nothing could stand in my way. I did pause briefly to sup on a cup of coffee—even a hunter needs nourishment. Then I resumed my search, armed with the sword of the Spirit, the shield of faith and the credit card of God's provision.

You see, I love things. They are one of the simple pleasures in life. Nice things, comfortable things. The things we own describe who we are. Nothing reveals a person like their CD collection and bookshelf. Things make me happy.

The Bible says that the eyes are the window to the soul. Trust me, the Bible is not wrong. With my eyes I see these things, and they seduce me. Sure, I don't need that Alessi sugar bowl, or one more shirt from Saba, or even that extra book to sit on my shelf till I get around to reading the other six sitting there.

It's an odd thing, desire. The lust of the flesh. It's not confined to sex; you can lust after a lot of different things. The perfect physique. The healthiest body. The best clothes. The nicest car. To be the most liked, the funniest, the most talented.

You can even lust after something seemingly more spiritual. To be the best preacher. To be a home cell leader. To be known as the most devoted person in your church.

Ask yourself why. Why do you want or need these things?

For me, it's all centred in our self-worth—who we think we are, and who we want to be. We all want to be loved, by our friends, by our partners, by total strangers. And we think that these little (and not so little) things make us more appealing, more attractive, better people.

But God loves you anyway, new Mossimo shirt or not.

Nothing can replace the peace of knowing God's love. Really knowing it. Money can't buy that.

Night Lights

Kel Richards

~

(John 14:1–4)

I am working the night-shift and walking home late,
And the streets are all empty and echo the scrape
Of my shoes as they scuff on the footpath and road;
In the silence I think of the people bestowed
In the comfort of warm beds and snuggled down deep
Who are drifting towards the sweet safety of sleep.

And I pull my coat closer and shiver inside
And I curse my old car and I wish I could ride.
But the garage said two days and now they say three
So I walk in the darkness, a cold refugee.
As I walk I see windows that glow from within
And I faintly hear voices—a soft, friendly din.

I imagine the lives that are lit by those lights
As they huddle around the oil heater tonight.
Are they happy or sad? Do they laugh? Do they cry?

These are things I can't guess. I'm a mere passer-by.
As I trudge in the darkness expecting a storm,
I know one thing: inside, in the light, they are warm!

I pass portraits of happiness, husband and wife,
Each window's a picture of warmness and life.
I remember the warm rooms that I have been in,
And I wish that I wasn't outside but within.
I can hear a night bird give a faint ghostly shriek;
The roadway around me is deserted and bleak.

A dog barks in a yard as I hurry on past,
In the darkness alone I am midnight's outcast.
Each window lights up like a panel of gold
And inside there is coffee and laughter untold.
There is light after light that is gleaming like chrome:
At the heart of the lights is the beat of a home.

There is longing for *Home* deep in everyone's breast,
And until we all find it we all have no rest.
'In my Father's house now there is many a room.'
So the Bible assures me, and so I assume.
There's a place in our heart for the place we desire,
Where the lights are turned on and the log's on the fire.

The Big Picture of Ken Duncan

Irene Voysey

~

The name Ken Duncan is synonymous with fine Australian photography. His Panographs®—panoramic photographs—have led thousands of people to appreciate the beauty of God's creation. Ken's testimony, like his photography, has an enduring beauty.

Ken first learned about photography at a Christian camp when he was just sixteen years old. That basic knowledge ignited such a passion in him that he commandeered his father's camera on his return home and from then on neglected schoolwork to take photographs.

At age twenty-two, Ken was no different from the majority of Australia's young adults. He wanted success. Turning his back on the Christian faith, even though his parents had spent time as missionaries with the Aboriginal people, he set off down the path of materialism.

By the time he turned thirty, Ken was financially successful and should have considered himself fulfilled. Instead he found himself seeking God while visiting Bali in Indonesia. Told by his guide that the name of Indonesia's tallest mountain, Mount Agung, means 'mountain of the gods', Ken decided to climb the mountain and challenge God. 'Show me who you are!' he demanded when he arrived at its summit. Although not yet the acclaimed photographer he is today, his photographs from that mountaintop broadened his vision, and Ken decided there had to be more to life than merely the pursuit of material things.

Following his return to Australia, his father suggested they visit some Aboriginal friends from his missionary days in the remote Kimberleys of Western Australia. Ken resigned from his job and went with his father, driven by his intense desire to discover 'the meaning of life'.

His time trekking in the wilderness with his father and their Aboriginal friends opened Ken up to the possibility of the spiritual realm. Startling confirmation of this came some months later when a friend died in his arms. Ken says, 'I felt his spirit leave his body as we tried to resuscitate him. At that point I knew there was a God and realised that I was spiritually bankrupt.'

He says, 'I decided that the Christian answer—repent, believe, receive—was too easy, and I pursued spirituality in Hinduism, Buddhism, Aboriginal spiritualism and many other beliefs. Through it all, my mother's prayers kept me from getting totally sucked into false teaching. Time and again, no matter how respected and famous the guru appeared to be, the Lord revealed to me the falseness of what I was being taught. Once, at Ayers Rock in Central Australia, I was in a really frightening situation in the Aboriginal spiritual realm and I called out, "God, help me!"—and he rescued me.'

But still Ken hadn't really submitted to God.

Not long after that episode, he developed gangrene and lay in a hospital bed, in danger of losing his foot. This time he said, 'Jesus, I've been running away for a long time. If you save me now, I promise not to run away again.'

Ken says, 'The Lord's presence was very real and for several days I enjoyed his closeness. But my old friends began to visit me, and once again I allowed myself to be led away by the distractions of the world. I left hospital missing only one toe.'

Later, on a visit to Tasmania, Ken developed hypothermia. He says, 'My mind had always been my strength, yet I found myself in a situation where my mind betrayed me and was telling me to just lie down. I was aware that obeying my mind would lead to my death. Again I cried out, "God, help me".'

Once again God was gracious. Ken says, 'He responded by filling me inside with a flash of great warmth. Later I learned the cure for hypothermia is to warm the patient from the inside, not from the outside. Again God had saved my life, but again I did not submit to his authority.'

Three months later he suffered a nervous breakdown. 'In the hospital there was a painting of Jesus wearing a crown of thorns,' he says. "That's me," I said to myself. "I'm pushing that crown of thorns onto his head." I'd finally reached the point where I was ready to promise I would never turn away again—and I meant it. I left that hospital the next day. A few weeks later my wife and I went to a church in our local area and both of us committed our lives to Christ.'

Ken remembers that throughout his search for God, the only Christians who made an impression on him were those who believed the Bible was true and were ready to defend that belief. He says, 'I had no time for Christians who said they believed one part of the Bible, but not another.' Nor could he deny the faith of his parents. He says simply, 'They lived it.'

Ken's favourite passage of Scripture is 'I can do everything through him [Christ] who gives me strength' (Philippians 4:13). Since he accepted Christ as his personal Lord and Saviour, Ken's rise to success in the world of photography has been spectacular. Acknowledged as among the world's leading panoramic specialists, he has numerous national and inter-national awards to his credit. The three Ken Duncan Galleries—one in Sydney at The Rocks, another in South-gate, Melbourne, and the third in Matcham, on the Central Coast of NSW—all display the Bible verse: 'For since the creation of the world, God's invisible qualities—his eternal power and divine nature—have been clearly seen, being understood from what has been made, so that men are without excuse' (Romans 1:20).

An Australian Elijah

John Blacket

~

In 1972, in the Aboriginal community of Elcho Island, there was a challenge in which it was understood by the people that the power of God was being pitted against the power of sacred stones from a *mindjalpi*, or sacred dilly bag. Aboriginal life stories tell how Aboriginal men stole a *mindjalpi* from the Djang'kawu sisters a long time ago. The Djang'kawu were two sisters who were spirit beings. They helped people relate to the land after its creation. One old man explained:

> *The dilly bag which belongs to the men in each mala [clan] is the proof that the mala has the authority over that land—because the dilly bag came from Djang'kawu.*

The issue of power and authority is very important, especially in how it is used. The *mindjalpi* is the basis for all their authority: for their discipline over young people and every member of the clan, so that their rules and customs are observed. But it can also be used for all sorts of other things,

206

such as to manipulate for personal gain.

In 1972, the whole community was gathered at Gali-win'ku for a concert at the school. During a traditional dance, one of the men dancing suddenly collapsed and died. Accusations and rumours spread quickly. *Galiwin'ku Church News* reported, 'Claims had been made that a certain small stone in one man's possession had the power to kill any person who touched it'.

Djiniyini Gondarra and Kevin Dhurrkay were Christian leaders at the time and were present for a fiery meeting on the oval on Sunday morning.

Djiniyini asked for the stone and, amidst protests from the crowd who feared for his safety, he held it and proceeded to witness to the power of Jesus Christ. He said that such objects have no power in themselves and that, if a person who touches it should become sick or even die, it is the great fear he had that is the cause. When asked if he had anything in his possession that possessed power, Djiniyini replied, 'Yes, I have the Bible!' After bearing his testimony, Kevin fearlessly picked up the much-feared objects which people had tipped out of their 'medicine bags' and he put them all back into their bags.

All this can be seen as preparation for the great revival among Aboriginal people that began in 1979. It was God rubbing sticks together to produce heat. He was blowing his breath on the dry twigs and leaves and a spark was lit that soon became a refining fire.

A Day at the MCG

Michael Frost

~

We find it simpler to see a church service as an expression of God's kingdom and a test match at the MCG as falling outside the kingdom. But let me put it to you this way: surely, a day at the MCG can be an entirely kingdom-like experience.

I know for many people a day at the cricket sounds horrible, but bear with me for the purposes of the argument. Imagine in the best possible scenario, a trip to an international cricket match in which the sense of well-being and personal nurture is at its greatest.

You attend with close friends who remind you of how greatly valued you are in this world. You enjoy a day of perfect weather, twenty-six degrees with a light nor'easter, and you are filled with a feeling of gratitude for God's good creation. There is fine food and wine to be shared and a camaraderie that speaks of personal security, intimacy and mutual trust.

For a Christian person whose eyes have been opened

by faith to God's creative agency—his kingdom, in this world—such a perfect day would be nothing short of a reminder and an intoxicating experience of God's grace, his rule, in the lives of the faithful. It occurs to me that this is entirely in keeping with the concerns of the kingdom: peace, love and hope.

Now let's consider another scenario: going to church. Imagine for a moment you go to church filled with a sense of bitterness and resentment toward someone who'll be there, maybe even the minister. Consider what it's like to go to church so filled with spite because the music is not as you'd have it or the preaching isn't interesting (or biblical or helpful) enough. Reflect on the impact of feeling alienated, rejected or betrayed by the people who attend the same church service.

The sense of defeat or anxiety or rage can be so debili-tating as to freeze you in apathy. Churches can be places where frightened and lazy people remain stuck in their fear and laziness. In other works, an experience many people consign to the realm of the sacred can in fact be operating in such a way as to limit the degree to which God's kingdom is encountered. And alternatively, an experience normally thought of as entirely temporal or profane can draw us closer to kingdom realities.

The King of Mintabi

Kerry Medway

~

$\mathcal{E}$ach month as part of my ministry I used to travel north from Coober Pedy and visit the Aboriginal Reserve and cattle stations, showing films and talking with lonely outback people.

I had heard of Mintabi, a boom opal-mining community, with the reputation of being a wild and unruly place into which no preacher dare venture. For a while I let stories of shootings and drunkenness postpone my visits to this place, but finally God made it clear that I could procrastinate no longer.

As I set out for Mintabi in fear and trepidation, miners in Coober Pedy warned me to be careful and watch out for a particular opal-miner named Ivan. He had the reputation of having murdered a number of people and had been banned from Coober Pedy opal-fields forever. I thanked my friends for this good news as I set out on the 350 kilometre drive to Mintabi, vowing to myself I wouldn't go near this man with 'a ten-foot pole'.

Whilst driving from Marla Bore to Mintabi, alone on a lonely track leading from the Stuart Highway west to this wild frontier community, I came upon a vehicle broken down. I stopped to offer a hand. Why I always stop in such circumstances I never know, as I know nothing about fixing cars apart from praying for them! As we talked and I lent him some spanners, I asked him his name. You guessed it. He was Ivan, the man I had been warned about. Here I was on a lonely track in the outback, with the very man I had hoped I would never meet!

Any minute I expected him to clobber me with my spanner and leave me for dead on the road. No matter how much I prayed, he couldn't get his car to go and so I offered to give Ivan a ride into Mintabi as his car (which was towing a tank of diesel fuel) was too heavy for my Subaru.

As we drove in, Ivan asked who I was and what I was doing coming into a place like Mintabi. I gulped and replied cautiously, 'I am a Christian minister and I'm coming to share Jesus and show some Christian films'. He said forcefully that he didn't go much on the 'Jesus bit', but no one had ever cared enough about the 100 men at Mintabi to come and show them pictures. To my amazement he was impressed and took me to the Mintabi restaurant, arranging with the barman to show my films there that evening.

My friend not only arranged the films, but said he would run around and invite the miners to come and see them. Well, let me tell you, when this guy invites you to anything, you just don't refuse! That night sixty-five tough opal-miners turned out to the local restaurant to watch Christian films.

They sat around the restaurant drinking beer and asking how many naked ladies there were going to be. I grinned and prayed, saying, 'You wait and see.'

The first film featured Johnny Cash in San Quentin Prison. They liked that and cheered after it had finished. The second film featured Billy Graham. Wow! Billy was only on the screen for thirty seconds before one opal-miner sprang to his feet, kicked a card table over and stormed out of the door, knocking it off its hinges. Another twenty-nine minutes to go! Somehow they went. Thankfully after that there were only a few mutterings and can-throwings and I continued to visit Mintabi every six weeks and show films to the men.

I discovered that although these miners were tough and lived and played rough, they were great guys underneath, needing Jesus like we all do. On a number of occasions after the films, I led some of them to a new faith in God.

He sure works in mysterious ways. The very man I was supposed never to meet was used by God to make me welcome and bring hope and new life to many men neglected and forgotten in the desert of outback Australia.

Whenever I visited Mintabi, I had a great friend in Ivan and often I would walk into the 'boozer' to talk with the men.

Butch, a former crocodile hunter, and some of the tough guys would give me a hard time, trying to goad me into a sick story or a filthy joke. You should have seen the look on their faces when Ivan, who ruled Mintabi by fear, walked into the boozer, patted me on the back and introduced me to a hushed crowd as his mate! How the temperature must have dropped—I am sure I saw some of the men begin to shiver and spill their beer!

A couple of times I visited around the camp sites walking into a caravan camp with my Bible tucked under my arm. As the men stared at me, I would quickly introduce myself, 'Hello, I'm Kerry, an Anglican priest. I have come to talk to you about God.' Their initial reaction to that introduction would quickly change when I added, 'I'm a mate of Ivan's.' That little sentence won a captive audience for a while and they always dutifully took any literature I left with them.

Once when I was at Mintabi, Ivan offered to take up a collection to help pay for the film rental. My usual practice was to ask for any donations. At Mintabi the men would pass around a beer carton or box in which to put their donations. They were very generous and obviously appreciated my visits and films.

This night the beer box had already been passed around. But Ivan looked into the box when it came back and exclaimed, 'These blokes are robbing you!' I said I was quite happy with whatever I was given and said that perhaps times were hard. 'No,' Ivan boomed, 'they are robbing you and I shall get some more money.' With that he grabbed the box and went around each man present, extracting extra money from them.

Ivan's method of extracting money was to grab hold of each man by the shirt and demand how much he had already put in. If Ivan considered that this was not enough, he would ask for more and, whatever he said, each man would put it in the box. As well as many men, there were two women present that night. One of the ladies Ivan grabbed by the throat and glared at her. She was so terrified that she emptied her *whole* purse into the collection box. Despite my embarrassment, Ivan collected quite a lot of extra money. And after that, whenever I returned with my films, the collection was always a healthy amount—the men (and women) obviously fearing another collection by Ivan.

I have often thought of hiring my Mintabi mate, Ivan, out to churches to assist them in taking up their Sunday collections. I am sure his method would reap a fortune in most city churches—if they could cope with him.

Basketball Games

Tim Costello

~∂

At the back of Melbourne's Collins Street Baptist Church there is an entrance by a longish lane-way between tall buildings, called Baptist Place. It runs between two wings of the Victoria Hotel; the hotel was built on land once owned by our church. There is a small court-yard at the end of the laneway, which has long been one of the CBD's major sites for young people to inject drugs.

Many of these started to come to our lunches, but another very life-giving thing we did at the time was to put up a basketball hoop right outside the back door. It changed the nature of what was previously just a shooting-up area so that it included a play area. For about eighteen months we played basketball most lunchtimes, and for street kids, even if they're stoned or angry or whatever, play is an important release. It actually brought laughter, life and a release of social energy right into the heart of the city. I loved it, and so did everyone who joined in with us.

215

In fact, play is important to all of us. I still play basketball in a Tuesday night competition, so it was great for me. Basketball is actually very physical; even though it is meant to be non-contact, you touch people, slap them and work up a sweat together, which is levelling. I liked to see the breakdown of that awful sense of people being charity objects in the company of a church minister. Of course, the kids were often better shots than I, and they put me down with great glee.

Deep down we all crave play. The tragedy for so many of these street kids is that they have grown up to be adults by the age of twelve. The adult world they learn is one which teaches them to trust no one and to expect only violence and abuse. This had crushed their childishness before they had been able to learn the ongoing role of play in life.

Ankle Bob

David R. Nicholas

~

Ankle Bob—pronounced this way by one of our offspring, but affectionately known to the whole congregation as 'Uncle Bob'—was a Yorkshireman born and bred. While he grew up in Yorkshire and lived first in Canada and then Australia, he never lost his accent.

For the first part of his life he was a bachelor. In his latter years he met a lady called Sadie, fell in love and married her. Together they managed a chicken farm way out in the countryside of New South Wales.

Their home was not fancy. To some it would have only been a glorified shed, yet the warmth of their love and hospitality saturated it. Many a missionary and many a minister and his wife spent happy days under their roof recuperating from the strain of service.

Bob and Sadie's home was a 'haven on the hill'. They had known the sorrow of a child that was stillborn, but rarely did they speak of this event. A bitter blow indeed, but they learned to lavish their love on the children of others.

Whatever Bob and Sadie did was always shared with their visitors. Feeding the fowls, collecting and cleaning the eggs ready for market, taking the eggs to market. All was co-operative effort. Anyone who stayed with them was considered part of what they were doing.

Their garden was also for the sharing.

Visitors were always treated to a garden tour. A special feature was inspecting the blooms Bob managed to cultivate. His speciality were schizanthus (the 'poor man's orchid'). His dahlias were beyond delight—massive blooms. As for his sweet peas, he surely had double the green fingers of the normal gardener. Furthermore, Ankle Bob always managed to have the pick of the crops in the district.

When the couple's visitors left, they were given blooms plus eggs or vegetables, because Bob and Sadie believed their produce was for sharing. They believed God had given them all they had and therefore they were to share his goodness with as many people as possible. Bob and his wife were not rich in this world's goods, but they shared what they had.

Even in church Bob, who was a deacon, always considered others, especially the minister. Bob attended an afternoon service and it was hard for him to stay awake during the sermon. When sermon time came round, rather than disturb anyone else, Bob quietly left his seat, went to the back of the church and stood during the sermon to stop himself falling asleep.

'Others' were the key fact of Bob's Christian life. The Bible instructs us to 'Share with God's people who are in need. Practise hospitality' (Romans 12:13). Ankle Bob followed this command in a most exact way.

My Version of Ecclesiastes 3:1-8

Amanda Smith

~

There's a time to do the dishes
 and a time to leave them in the sink.

There's a time to save Grandma's lace tablecloth for
 Christmas dinner
and a time to use it for breakfast on Tuesday morning.

There's a time to say, 'Don't bother me now, I'm busy',
and a time to drop everything to roll around the floor with
 your kids,
dance around the living room with your husband or stop
 for a cuppa with a friend.

There's a time to race out late at night to return the video
and a time to stay at home with your family and pay the
 late fee.

There's a time to nag your husband about wasting film
and a time to let him snap as many photos as he wants of
his little girl in her first ballet costume.

There's a time to say, 'Save those for the guests',
and a time to let your husband take the best biscuit from
the batch.

There's a time to say, 'Don't spill that on the couch!'
and a time to let your son make a fort with the couch
cushions.

God has made every thing beautiful in its time.

Cat Bites Man

David R. Nicholas

In the journalistic world there is an old saying: 'When a man bites a dog it's news.' There was a new twist to this theme when an Australian was bitten by his cat. This man took the cat to a vet, and assisted him while the cat was on the operating table. The feline suddenly snapped at one of his fingers, and, as a result, part of the finger had to be amputated. A legal battle followed, during which the cat owner claimed the vet had not properly secured the cat on the table. The case concluded with the wounded man receiving a considerable damages payout.

How complicated a simple event can become. One small thing can grow large. A little act can start a chain of events. Sometimes we find it hard to imagine the final results of what we do. Minor deeds of kindness can multiply as we share with others the little we have. Our influence can be far more powerful than we think.

Leslie Flynn tells how a soldier in a military hospital asked the chaplain to send a message to his Sunday school teacher: 'Tell her I die a Christian and have never forgotten her teaching.' The chaplain wrote to the teacher and three weeks later received this reply:

May God have mercy on my soul. Only last month I resigned my Sunday school class, feeling my teaching never did much good. Scarcely had I given up my class when your letter arrived, telling me my teaching had been the means of winning a pupil to Christ. I have gone back to my pastor and told him I will try again in Christ's name to be faithful to the end.

While we tend to overlook minor deeds, our Lord is able to take them, transforming them into major ones.

Jack Goldsmith—Outback Legend

Nathan Brown

He's been a ringer, boundary rider, trapper, buffalo shooter, horse breaker, road-train driver, boxing troupe fighter, wharfie, bottle and brick collector and timber cutter. Now, sixty-six years of age and retired in northern New South Wales, bushman Jack Goldsmith is also a proud member of the Stockman's Hall of Fame, located at Longreach, Queensland.

Perhaps more notably, given the Australian psyche, in a peculiarly Australian tribute, *Stockman's Hall of Fame* magazine described him as 'the last of the old-time, dinky-di cattle duffers'.

Jack was born in the Blue Mountains west of Sydney, and was only four when his mother died. An aunt cared for him until his father remarried. The new family arrangement wasn't a happy one for Jack, and he went through a time of abuse—physical and mental—from his stepmother, 'and others that I care not to mention,' he says.

He left home at sixteen and 'I headed for the back country' of western New South Wales. After spending time rabbit trapping, Jack worked his way north to Queensland when, soon after, the Korean War broke out. He joined the regular army—'When I was old enough'—hoping to see some action. The war ended before he was able to leave Australia, so, he says, 'I shot through,' and headed further north.

'I always wanted to be a ringer—a stockman,' he explains. 'I went boundary riding near Boulia, in south-western Queensland, and worked on a number of stations around Cloncurry. Next I cut timber around the Atherton Tableland for awhile, but eventually headed to the Gulf [of Carpentaria]. And that's where I stayed for the next twelve years.'

There he worked on the huge cattle stations of the region, where he learned to break horses. He soon earned a reputation for both breaking horses and as a brawler. 'Around Normanton, I got into a few fights, and then your reputation goes ahead of you—more than what you really deserve. By the time they finish talking about you in various hotel bars and the different towns around the Gulf, you're a world-beater. Your name grows, especially if you fight and beat somebody who's got a big reputation.'

Eventually Jack bought a one-third share in a small property in the Gulf area. The station was stocked with unbranded cattle, mostly duffed (stolen) from bigger neighbours. But, Jack says, there's a strict code of honour among cattle thieves: 'In the cattle-duffing business, you're not frowned upon when you're taking from the big stations. I took 300 in one hit once and it never worried my conscience at all. But if I took one beast off a battler, that would be wrong.

'Cattle duffing is really a trade. You don't do stupid things like interfering with brands; that's outright stealing,' he says, 'but we never used to eat our own beef. There's an old saying in the back country: If you want to know what your own beef tastes like, go to your neighbour's for dinner. It was the generally done thing.'

At that time, cattle duffing was somewhat more acceptable. Jack remembers how, in Queensland, when cattle duffers came to court, they were looked upon with high esteem because a lot of the jury were themselves former duffers. 'It was very hard to convict someone of cattle duffing in the old days,' he says.

These days he sees things differently. 'That [it was acceptable] doesn't make it right; stealing is stealing. And, it's different these days. I have no sympathy for those who do it with trucks and indiscriminately.' But after four years of cattle duffing he had second thoughts. 'All we did was cattle duffing, but it got us nowhere. All I got out of it was excitement.'

It's excitement you feel as you listen to Jack's many stories of exploits in Australia's wildest, most dangerous areas. For instance, he once swam a crocodile-infested river simply to avoid being labelled a coward after he'd failed to show up for a big fight. Three days later a huge crocodile took a bullock at the point where he'd set out on the 200 metre swim. There are stories of shoot-outs and stampedes and more—raw material of Australia's heritage and the stuff of romance and legend.

Having lived the bush life, Jack is now proud to be included in the Stockman's Hall of Fame. Although the heritage centre is situated some 1200 kilometres north-west of Brisbane and 700 kilometres inland, Jack usually goes back for the annual get-together.

'The Hall of Fame is something Australia really needs,' he says. 'It's keeping our heritage alive. I love going to the Hall, and I've made some great friends there. Memories come rushing back when you go through it. It's a life I loved, and I just love that part of our heritage.'

Despite his great affection for the bush and the life of his past, Jack acknowledges there are things he doesn't miss. The uncertainty of life in the back country, for example. And its weather. In fact, it was bad weather that changed his life.

'We were mustering bullocks on a small station out from Charters Towers,' he recounts, 'and unseasonal rain blew in. We'd generally take our packhorses out to this place to muster, staying for about three weeks. However, this time, we took the truck out and we got caught. The rivers rose and we couldn't move. We started running out of food—we had plenty of beef, of course, but we had nothing to do. The only thing we had to read was the Northern Queensland Telephone Directory.

Everyone knew every saddler, every butcher, every station!

'So when I got back to the station, I said next time we went out, I'd take plenty to read. At the station there were plenty of old *Reader's Digests*, so I took one. In it was an advertisement for a Bible prophecy study correspondence course, which I sent away for. I did the course, and it was the dawning of a new experience.

'I gave up swearing straight away. It was a strange feeling,' he remembers. 'I didn't know at the time, but it was God beginning to change my life.'

After another two years working on stations around Charters Towers, Jack moved to Sydney with his wife. Adapting to city life was a challenge, yet he kept working through the Bible lessons and studying the Bible. The couple soon began to search for a church to attend and investigated a number of different denominations.

Then, while breaking horses near Nowra, NSW, in 1967, Jack met a former minister of the Seventh-day Adventist Church who he spoke with at length. When he returned to Sydney, he found the address of the local church and wrote them a letter. As he remembers it, his letter asked something like: 'Why do you mob go to church on Saturday and not Sunday? And why don't you eat meat?'

A Seventh-day Adventist minister dropped by their North Sydney flat and together they began to study the Bible. 'I soon knew I'd found what I was looking for,' Jack says.

This was a turning point in his life. Since then he's been actively involved in his church and shares his faith with enthusiasm. But he's always amazed as he looks back on the episodes of his bush life at how often he can see God's care and love for him, although he didn't recognise it, not at the time.

He loves the bush—the back country—still: 'It's where my heart is,' he says fondly. 'The only reason I'm not there now is that when I go back, everybody expects me to be down the pub brawling! And you want to go to church, but it's always too far away.'

He still visits it regularly, however. 'As I said to a lady once—it won't work between you and me, 'cause I've got another woman, and every now and then I go visit her. Her name is Back Country. I just can't keep away from her. I go out there and roll my swag out under a tree. I can be out there in my swag and by myself looking up at the stars, yet never be lonely.'

Lonely? Not with God so close and so obvious in nature and the heavens. It's a part of the Australian legend and heritage, the mateship and camaraderie of the back country, that provides Jack with a unique perspective on God. 'Not only is Jesus the Creator and our Redeemer, he's also our Mate. And the definition of a mate is someone who knows all the bad things about us, but still remains your friend.'

The Shared Meal

Tim Costello

~

In my own home, we still try to have some family meals with the television off, and to use the time for sharing news and concerns. Many people make a shared meal an opportunity to pray, saying grace, lighting a candle, holding hands or allowing a short period of meditation before beginning to eat. It is easy to think of ways in which we can enrich a meal's quality with a little ritual, but I wonder if it may be about to completely lose its power with the onslaught of fast food. Most of the people in my audiences tell me that, what with casual work and television, 'you can forget family meals'.

I suppose it's a mark of my desperation that now I find myself addressing the young woman in the local McDonald's by name when she serves our family's orders. Well, the staff at McDonald's have their first names on a label, so aren't we supposed to talk to them?

One time I asked 'Karen' about how her day had been and whether she was enjoying work. She looked stunned and curious. My kids looked embarrassed. Afterwards my daughter took me aside and said, 'If you do that once more, I'll never come out to eat with you ever again'. So I asked, 'Well, why has she got a name tag on if I'm not meant to use it?' I was told that she has a name tag so that if she 'stuffed up' we would know who to report! Apparently, performance has replaced identity and chattiness. It is hard for those of us brought up on the friendly meal ritual, but I realise now that, in being familiar with Karen, I am breaking some deeply felt taboo.

When I had ordered Karen said, 'There'll be a two-minute wait for the burger, sir'. Before I could stop myself I asked, 'Why's that?', recalling that McDonald's advertises instant service. She explained that the time was for cooking the food. I almost said, 'Why are you cooking the food?' Then I realised with a shock that not only are we losing the ritual of eating together, but I was even starting to forget that there are still certain rituals in the preparation of a hamburger! No wonder in some parts of the world there is the growth of a new movement called 'slow food' which celebrates the enchantment of the time spent cooking and eating. Losing time which can be available for preparation and participation in our rituals means that as soul-searchers we are losing the time to savour the recipes for life, the exquisite choice of choosing a good one, and the careful shopping for the right ingredients.

But my most cherished shared meals are taken in the basement at the back of our church, where sometimes I see the face of a street person come alive as he or she sits at our table. Without the dehumanising label of 'drug addict', I can see the ancient magic of a shared meal start to work, and tongues begin to loosen. I hear about Leon who used to eke out a living as a back-up barber until his clients told him his stories were so good he should go on the stage. Now he's getting gigs as a stand-up comedian in pubs. Or I listen to the stories of someone like Danny, with his olive skin, ponytail and dishevelled appearance from the long nights spent in a disused car on a vacant block of land in the city. He put up a notice which advertised the vacant lot as a $5 all-day carpark, gave his customers used tickets discarded from other carparks, and was doing so well that he employed two other street people in the business. Overnight he went from being unemployed to having a job, and being an employer! His time with us seemed even to reawaken some of his values: he refused to charge mums or old people. Unfortunately the owner of the empty lot caught up with the workings of this 'goldmine', and Danny has made himself scarce.

People like Leon and Danny are certainly outsiders, even on the edge of the law, but my staff come to know and love them, and that is thanks to the ritual of our shared meal. We find wholeness through hospitality, through listening to the pain and joy of the other.

God's Marbles

Ken Duncan

~

If you travel down the Stuart Highway from Tennant Creek to Alice Springs, you'll soon come upon a strange collection of hundreds of boulders, some as big as houses, strewn across a spinifex valley in imposing and even impossible positions. Made of granite and rounded by erosion and flaking, their official name, the 'Devil's Marbles', implies a diabolical origin—as if the devil had thrown them down with mischievous carelessness. I prefer to think of them as the handiwork of a Creator who does nothing haphazardly, and I'm endeavouring to have them renamed 'God's Marbles' to give credit where credit is due.

The Tale of Stumpy and Slick

Barry Chant

~

Slick was the biggest grain in the bin. And he knew it.

'Why,' he said to himself, 'I have enough potential in me to feed the whole world.'

'What was that?' asked Husky, another grain, lying near him in the bin.

'Oh, nothing,' said Slick. 'Just talking to myself.'

'But you said something about the whole world,' Husky went on.

'Well, yes,' Slick admitted. 'I did say something like that. I was just thinking that, given enough time, of course, you or I could produce enough grain to fill the whole world.'

'The whole world?' replied Husky incredulously.

'Think about it,' said Slick. 'Each year we can multiply. Next year there could be fifty just like you or me. The next year there would be 2500. The next year 125,000. And then 6,250,000. And so on. Within ten years we could produce 94,656,250,000,000,000 grains each!'

'Wow!' said Husky. 'As many as that? I never realised we could do that much!'

'In fact, you or I could produce a whole barn full of grain on our own,' Slick continued. 'A factory full of bread. We could even be the solution to world malnutrition! We have the potential for life!'

And the more he thought about it, the more excited Slick became. He wormed his way to the edge of the bin and sat there glowing.

'Hey, you blokes,' he shouted. 'We've got something really great to share. We have a message of salvation for the whole world! We can change the face of the earth! But we must believe it. We must confess it. We must talk about it to one another. And we can do it!'

There was a stirring in the bin. The other grains began to murmur excitedly among themselves. 'He's right, you know . . . We've really got to believe this . . . It's time someone presented a positive approach . . . Imagine! World-changing power in our hands!' And so on.

In the process of all this, one shrivelled-up little grain was pushed over the edge of the bin into the ground.

'Hey! Stumpy!' called Slick. 'What are you doing down there? Why don't you stay in the bin with the rest of us?'

'Not my fault!' shouted Stumpy. 'You pushed me out!'

But his words were lost to the excited crowd in the bin. Soon they were singing songs about life and vigour and growth and miracles and changing the world.

They talked about all the great things they could do. They spoke to each other about the enormous potential that lay within them. 'Why,' they said, 'We can do anything through the life that is within us.'

Stumpy lay there listening to all the celebration. 'What am I going to do?' he lamented. 'How can I ever get back to the bin?' He felt very lonely.

Then something else happened that was even worse. A farmhand walking by kicked the ground with his heavy boot. A clod of dirt, dust and straw shot into the air—and so did Stumpy.

'Oh!' he cried as he spun dizzily around. 'What will happen to me now?'

He hit the ground with a thud. He lay there bruised and winded. The sounds of the grain in the bin could be heard no more. All was silent and he felt so alone.

'Poor old Stumpy,' said Slick, when he saw him being kicked away. 'He's really lost his reputation now.'

It was Slick's policy always to gather the right people around him. So when he saw Stumpy covered in grime and dust, Slick turned away. ('Never get your hands dirty,' he said to himself. 'That's my motto. Always delegate. Let someone else do the menial tasks. I need to concentrate on the high calling I have. I must make full use of my gifts.')

But worse was to happen yet to poor Stumpy. There was a

roaring and a whistling and a rumbling; and before he knew what was going on, he found himself jammed into the tread of a tyre on the farmer's car, being whizzed around at a furious rate. 'Oh, oh, oh,' he whined, dizzy and sick. 'What now?'

Suddenly, with a flick, he rocketed out from the tyre into the dusty air. He held himself tense waiting to bounce on the hard ground. Instead, to his immense relief, he landed with a quiet 'plop' in the soft earth of a ploughed paddock.

A few minutes later, however, a wandering cow trod on him, pushing him deep into the ground. Surrounded by darkness and crushed into the soil, Stumpy died of a broken heart.

Slick, meanwhile, was really enjoying life. Since he had begun to talk about the future goals of the bin, a new spirit of purpose and direction had emerged. The ten-year plan he had first mentioned was being worked out in detail, and in fact, it now appeared that even greater heights could be reached.

'If we set progressive goals and plan carefully,' Slick told his eager companions, 'we can actually reach a ten-year target of an extra one billion each. Imagine that!'

There was an excited murmur and then someone began to applaud. Soon there was prolonged cheering and shouting. They could not even count the ultimate, combined result!

By this time, Slick had forgotten Stumpy altogether. In any case, he would not have exchanged places with him for anything. Here he was, popular, surrounded by friends and gaining in standing every day. His self-image was constantly being bolstered and his achievements feted by all. Most of the time now he felt that warm, glowing feeling that comes from being admired and well-liked.

'I would just like to say to every one of you,' he declared one day in a speech, 'how much I appreciate the support and encouragement I have received. I could not have done what I have done without your help and assistance. In particular, I would like to express my appreciation to Husky, who first helped me develop my theories.'

Everyone applauded and whispered to each other about Slick's humility and generosity.

Suddenly, without warning, there was an enormous shaking and banging. The whole bin was lifted, twisted and turned upside-down. Grains were thrown against one another in chaos and confusion. There were screams and cries of panic. And then the great slide began. First it was those on the outer. Then more and more joined the move until it became an avalanche. There was nothing any of them could do. Out of the bin and into a truck they went, a helpless, tumbling mass.

'What's happened?' Slick asked himself in panic. 'What are they doing to us? Where are we going? Don't they know about our plans to save the world?'

Then his voice was lost in a smother of dust and grain and he lay coughing and choking in the middle of the pile.

Well, soon they were at the flour mill and it was only a matter of time before Slick and Husky and all the rest were ground to powder, baked into bread and eaten by a bunch of school kids at a barbecue. But while all this was going on, something rather special and exciting was happening to Stumpy.

Out of his broken heart, a small white shoot began to appear. It snuggled its way through the dark brown earth, probing and searching until finally it poked its head out through the warm, sun-blessed surface of the ground.

The white changed to green and continued to reach upwards, seeking the sun and its life-giving power. The green strengthened and grew large, with broad leaves appearing on either side. And then, new grain began to appear at the head, full and rich and pregnant with life.

And as the days passed, it changed colour again, now becoming rusty and brown. And in the head was—Stumpy? No, for Stumpy was dead. But there in his place were dozens of others like him—indeed, more than like him, for some were like Slick and Husky, fuller and richer. Out of one shrivelled, small grain who had died had come multiplied life.

Everything that Slick had said was right, of course. It was just that he had forgotten one thing.

'Unless a kernel of wheat falls into the ground and dies, it remains only a single seed. But if it dies, it produces many seeds. The man who loves his life will lose it, while the man

who hates his life in this world will keep it for eternal life'
(John 12:24–25).

THERE IS NO RESURRECTION
WITHOUT CRUCIFIXION

The Whales

Michael Frost

~

Some years ago, a couple of southern right whales were spotted off the coast of Sydney. These magnificent creatures are rare in such waters so there was quite a fuss made of them by those who concern themselves with ocean life. They were made welcome by beach users and so proceeded to loll their way up the coast, calling in on just about every Sydney beach on their way.

I was astounded by the response of such a busy, cynical city as Sydney to these animals. Each headland they passed on their slow and casual journey north was crammed with sightseers aiming their cameras and binoculars at the big black objects in the water. It occurred to me that the two weeks we spent watching them, with every evening news broadcast following their every move, was just like a great collective sigh. We needed our breath to be taken away. We needed an awe experience to elevate us from our jaded self-centred belief that we are the masters of the universe.

Those two whales reminded us that there are greater, more awesome realities than our own. You watch, next time you visit your local zoo, which animals are the most popular; without exception they are the great and frightening creatures like the big cats, the elephants and bears, the crocodiles and alligators. This is because we need to observe a creature that reminds us of our inadequacy. It gives us the message that we are not the ultimate power, that there are creatures bigger and stronger than ourselves, creatures we didn't make and who are not subject to our control. Of course, the irony is that they are caged and docile. But our souls are often starved for that sense of awe, that encounter with grandeur that helps us find our real place in the universe.

Off the Back of a Truck

Margaret Reeson

Serenity Farm was a place in the country where homeless and desti-tute people could go to restore their self-confidence. However, money was always tight.

'We've got our seed potatoes!' Tony was jubilant. 'We've been praying about it together for a while—well, the other super-visors and I have been praying and a few of the guys half believed in it. But God has answered our prayers and the fellows are impressed.'

He told the story. He had been out driving with a few of the men in the Farm car along a country road. They were following a truck, and he noticed that it was loaded with sacks of potatoes. As the truck rounded a corner, the load started to shift and bags of potatoes began to fall onto the road. The truck stopped.

Tony thought, 'Well, Lord, perhaps that's your answer to our prayer,' so he pulled off the road and went to offer the driver help with reloading the potatoes. Gratefully, the driver agreed and they worked together. Some of the bags had burst, spilling potatoes across the road. The driver looked at the scattered potatoes.

'I'm not going to worry about those,' he said.

'Could we have them then? We want some for planting.'

'Suit yourself. You're welcome to them. But these are A grade new potatoes and you can't grow those. See if you can swap them for seed potatoes.'

Tony and the men collected all the loose potatoes, loaded them into the car and took them to their local greengrocer who exchanged them for seed potatoes. The potatoes were now safely in the ground.

Tony finished his story. 'It's had quite an impact,' he said. 'Some of those guys have become Christians at services at the Mission and then they've come out here. They see us praying about real things, trusting God to help us with the practical things of living, not just some sort of vague religious theory. They say that they are not going to forget this answer to prayer—our spuds that fell off the back of a truck!'

Carols by Candlelight

Mal Garvin

~

The camera zooms into the softly lit face of the sleeping child; the candles flicker like glow worms across the vast crowd sitting tight packed on the lawns at the Sidney Myer Music Bowl. Across the nation families sit together, drawn into the drama and intimacy of Australia's best-known 'Carols by Candlelight', a vast community event of the nation marking the birth of a child.

The idea of 'Carols by Candlelight', uniquely suited to the summer season of the southern hemisphere, was born in 1937 when a Melbourne radio broadcaster, Norman Banks, was walking home after a shift. It was Christmas Eve. He said, 'I was walking past a house in St Kilda Road and through the window I saw an elderly lady in bed. There was a candle and a radio beside her and she was singing "Away in a Manger". I was enthralled. It really gave me an idea of what Christmas is all about. I thought if one old lady could do that, what about a thousand people?'

So, on 24 December 1938, several thousand people gathered in Melbourne's Alexandra Gardens for the first ever 'Carols by Candlelight'.

The outreach of World War 2 strengthened the community's resolve to celebrate Christmas, and through those dark years people gathered every Christmas Eve until, a month after the end of the war in 1945, they gathered with a sense of joy and thankfulness. Norman Banks said, 'The 1945 Carols sent a shiver up and down your spine.'

Over the years the tradition spread—across Victoria, across Australia and across the world. Today, all over the country, towns and suburbs have their 'Carols by Candlelight' where hundreds or even thousands gather on ovals and lawns, each holding a lighted candle and singing the songs of Christmas.

These celebrations built on earlier traditions. As early as 1865, Cornish miners in Moonta, South Australia, accustomed to Carol Singers trudging around their Cornish villages, used to gather on the flats or the loading platforms at the mine for the shortened Christmas Eve shift and there they would break out in song. Their carols (which they pronounced 'curls') were sung to the light of Fat Jacks—big, fat, tallow candles stuck on the front of their safety hats with dabs of damp clay. The mine shift supervisors would turn a blind eye to these Christmas celebrations. So right there, in the midst of the mine and the rubble, work-hardened miners lifted their hearts and voices and brought some light and joy into the darkness.

Every year Australians now sing and celebrate the birth of a baby whose arrival signalled to the world that God was with us. And that is as true today as it was 2000 years ago. The child who divided history into BC and AD was the visible statement by the Creator of his nature and his compassion for humankind. He was the child who brought hope to the world.

As we sing carols each year and watch the candles flickering in the darkness, it assures us that God is with us.

Better than Gold

Gordon Moyes

～

When I was a teenage athlete, my athletics club had the opportunity to purchase tickets for the 1956 Melbourne Olympic Games before they went on sale to the general public. I gathered all the money I could to buy tickets for every day of the athletics. I got seats in the Great Southern Stand of the MCG, directly in line with the finish line. During those Olympics, I watched Australia's 'golden girl', Betty Cuthbert, win three gold medals in the 100 metres, 200 metres and 4 × 100 metres relay.

As a young athlete, good enough to get into state competition but not good enough to get into national or international competition, I watched carefully everyone I admired. I admired Betty Cuthbert. She was eight months older than I was. I never realised that we would become close friends years later.

Over the seven years following the 1956 Olympics, Betty set sixteen world records for running. However, at the Rome

Olympics in 1960 she was suffering from a torn hamstring and was eliminated early from competition, and also had to scratch from the 200 metres event for which she was favourite. In 1964 at the Tokyo Olympics she defied a dislocated bone in her foot and switched to the 400 metres event, winning her fourth gold medal in a race she described as the 'only perfect race I have ever run. Though I thanked God after crossing the finish line, it was my secret,' she said. 'I was embarrassed at the time.'

From this same period of time, I conducted evangelistic crusades around Australia, often in country towns where I preached the gospel, calling people to commitment to Christ. I preached in over 400 such crusades. Not long ago Betty was featured in the INPHO recorded telephone service in which she recounted the highlights of her life. Having mentioned the athletic highlights, she told of a night in 1985 when, burdened by her sin, she attended a mission in the Lismore Town Hall at which I was the evangelist. Betty said, 'Dr Moyes told how we each must lay aside "the sin which holds onto us so tightly" and commit our lives to Christ. He said, "There are private practising Christians here." I was compelled to go forward and prayed to receive Jesus as my Lord and Saviour. Now I try to share the good news of Jesus with as many people as possible.'

I remember the scene vividly. When I gave the appeal Betty came to the front before anyone else. I recognised her instantly. After counselling her, we kept in contact and she frequently came to Wesley Mission and appeared on my television and radio programs.

That is how I came to know she had contracted multiple sclerosis. We prayed together and I gave her encouragement and support. She told a *Sydney Morning Herald* reporter in 1996: 'We all live with faith. You have faith sitting in that blooming chair that it won't collapse under you. A lot of people think born-again Christians are loopy. I don't mind that, but I wish they would take time to find out what it means.' Betty was no longer a secret Christian. She told everyone of the need to have faith in Christ.

In the 2000 Sydney Olympics I was again sitting in the stands. I was greatly moved at the Opening Ceremony when the first athlete into the arena with the Olympic torch was Betty Cuthbert. The 125,000 people present roared their approval. She was in her wheelchair because today she is wheelchair-bound. She was assisted by Australian athlete and Olympic silver medallist Raelene Boyle.

Just shortly before, she had told a packed church about how we had met, and about the most important thing in her life, her friendship with Jesus Christ. And she told everyone that they too could not remain secret Christians.

The Rich Treasure of Forgiveness

Kel Richards

~

Kitty Djosy was a Jewish woman who lived in Budapest, Hungary, during World War 2. After suffering at the hands of the Nazis, she eventually went on to make a new life in Australia. There, in 1972, she finally found her life-long hunger for peace and belonging was satisfied by faith in Jesus.

In January 2001, Kitty Djosy attended the annual Summer School run by the Church Missionary Society at the Katoomba Convention Centre, west of Sydney. She went with her friend Betty Powell— Betty's husband Ken having died the previous year. Their accommodation was in the CMS Centre, and as she struggled through the gate with her bag and dooner Kitty heard a woman's voice saying, 'Here, let me help you with that.'

'No, no I can manage,' Kitty replied, but the younger woman insisted. Kitty noticed that she had a European accent.

'Where are you from?'

'Germany, originally.'

The young woman introduced herself as Hanna Collison. Later Kitty discovered that Hanna and her husband Max (with their three children Tim, Katrin and John) were CMS missionaries in Kenya.

'We must have a proper talk together,' said Kitty, 'a real talk—before Summer School is over.'

Hanna readily agreed.

In the busy days that followed, Kitty discovered that Max and Hanna Collison worked in the slums of Nairobi where Max had established a network of self-supporting clinics where even the poorest slum dwellers could receive medical treatment. By using enthusiastic Christian volunteers, costs were kept to a minimum.

'Without the volunteers,' Max explained to Kitty, 'the clinics would never have opened, and could not remain open. As it is, we haven't had to close one single day due to lack of volunteers. They pack the drugs, talk to patients, and do many of the administrative and practical tasks. The clinics don't depend on me. They are entirely self-supporting and reproducible.'

Over the next few days Kitty came to know the Collisons well, as they too were staying at the CMS Centre.

'Don't forget, we must make time to have good talk—a proper talk,' Kitty said to Hanna, 'before Summer School is over.'

'Yes,' responded Hanna enthusiastically, 'we must do that.'

But it was a busy week, and they didn't get together for that talk until their very last meal together.

That last night they sat in the dining room and began to talk about themselves and their backgrounds.

'I was born in Budapest,' said Kitty. 'What about you?'

'Essen—in western Germany,' Hanna replied, 'that's where I was born and grew up.'

Kitty went on to explain about growing up Jewish in Hungary, about losing every male member of her family in the death camps during World War Two, and about some of the horrors she, herself, had experienced. As she did so Hanna froze.

Hanna Collison felt that sudden hollow feeling in the pit of the stomach that comes when something has to be confronted that has been avoided for a long time.

The history of the Second World War and the holocaust haunted Hanna, even though it had all happened before she was born. Her father had been a soldier in Hitler's SS— compelled to join when he turned eighteen. He had been a foot soldier during the advance into Poland in 1939. In January 1941 he was seriously wounded, and took no further active part in the war.

As Hanna had learned the history of those years she had always assumed that her father had never personally done anything wrong. He was a gentle, softly spoken man—and he was Hanna's beloved father—and she believed him incapable of the atrocities she heard and read about. He never talked about the war. He had been very young, had been invalided out of the SS early in the conflict, and the memories of that time were, clearly, too painful for him to discuss.

But even if there was no direct guilt in her family Hanna was intensely aware of what her country had done, and what misery her nation had inflicted on so many. Essen, where she grew up, was a major industrial city where many of the armaments and weapons were manufactured for Hitler during the Second World War.

Now, she was facing a woman who had suffered at German hands in World War Two.

This was the first time Hanna had ever met a Jewish man or woman of that war generation. She was convinced that no Jewish person could ever forgive a German for what had happened. All of this was running rapidly through Hanna's mind as Kitty spoke.

She felt the colour drain out of her face.

When Kitty had finished speaking Hanna said quietly, 'Then you must not like me. I am German by birth. It was my country that did all of those things to your family.'

'Not at all!' Kitty cried. 'You are my sister in Christ and I love you. When I became a Christian I forgave everything that had ever happened to me or my family. You mustn't feel that way. We are together, we are sisters, there is no barrier between us.'

Then both women had tears in their eyes. A moment later they were hugging and weeping. Hanna felt that Kitty's words were a gift from God—liberating her from a lifetime of guilt and concern over the suffering her country, her people, had inflicted. She had long known, from the Bible, God's gracious and generous forgiveness—but now she *felt* forgiven. She wanted to shout it from the housetops. She wanted to hurry back to Kenya to share the experience with a fellow missionary, a woman from the former East Germany, who carried the same burden.

Kitty and Hanna were no longer German and Jew—they were one in Jesus Christ.

Kitty had found the place where the human heart finds rest. She had found forgiveness. And in that forgiveness she had found a rich treasure she could share.

Credits

'Granny Smith—A Parable of Australia' by Mal Garvin is from
   Us Aussies (updated edition, Croydon, NSW: Hayzon/Fusion
   Australia, 1992), pp. 154–5.

'Waiting for Rainbows' by Ken Duncan is from *America Wide*
   (Ken Duncan Panographs, 2001).

'Walk with Me' by Jim Stallard is adapted from *God's Quad* (Kew, Vic.:
   Christian Blind Mission International, 2000), pp. 112–14.

'Shout to the Lord!' by Camerin Courtney is adapted from *Today's
   Christian Woman*, March/April 2001.

'The House With No Steps', © 2001 Gordon Moyes.

'The Murrumbidgee' by Michael Frost is from *Eyes Wide Open*
   (Sutherland, NSW: Albatross Books, 1998), pp. 69–71.

'Never Give Up' by Betty Cuthbert is adapted from *Golden Girl*
   (Sydney: Strand Publishing, 2000), pp. 38–9, 128–9.

'Balaam's 21st Century Ass' by Phillip Jensen is from *Southern Cross*,
   May 2000.

'Parliament My Parish' by Fred Nile is condensed from *Fred Nile:
   An Autobiography* (Sydney: Strand Publishing, 2001), pp. 150–4.

'Lady of Leisure' by Angela Eynaud is from *Alive Magazine*,
 Nov. 1999, p. 16.

'The Bus Fare' by Pat Mesiti is from *Dreamers Never Sleep* (Sydney:
 Self published, 1996), pp. 87–8.

'Jesus—Friend of Prostitutes' by Tim Costello is from *Streets of Hope*
 (Sydney: Allen & Unwin/Albatross Books, 1998), pp. 17–19.

'The Body of Christ' by Margaret Reeson is from *Whereabouts Unknown*
 (Sutherland: Albatross Books, 1993), pp. 210–11.

'The Ballad of the Two Sons', © 2001 Kel Richards. All fourteen of
 Kel Richards' *Bush Ballards* are available on CD from your local
 bookshop or direct from the publisher on (02) 9427 4197 or
 beacon@planet.net.au

'Comfort or Convictions?' by Steve Grace is from *Milestones, Mistakes
 and Miracles*, a forthcoming book. For details see Steve's website
 (www.stevegrace.com).

'The Battlefield of the Mind' by Margaret Court is adapted from
 Winning Words (Sydney: Strand Publishing, 1999), pp. 22–5.

'Tears of God' by Michael Frost is from *Eyes Wide Open* (Sutherland,
 NSW: Albatross Books, 1998), p. 145.

'The Newcastle Freeway', © 2001 Gordon Moyes.

'Sunday Night Live in St Kilda' by Tim Costello is from *Streets of Hope*
 (Sydney: Allen & Unwin/Albatross Books, 1998), pp. 88–90.

'You've Got Mail' by Phil Gibbons is adapted from *Outreach*, Sep./Oct.
 1999, p. 14.

'What Will I Give My Kids?', © 2001 Glenn Williams. Glenn is the
 founder and CEO of Focus on the Family Australia, an organisation

257

dedicated to strengthening Australia's families. For more information please visit their website (www.fofa.com.au).

'Overcoming Fears' by Ken Duncan is from *America Wide* (Ken Duncan Panographs, 2001).

'When You're Going Through Hell, Don't Stop' by Pat Mesiti is from *Dreamers Never Sleep* (Sydney: Self published, 1996), pp. 185–7.

'Dream House' by Angela Eynaud is from *Alive Magazine*, May 2001, p. 19.

'A Boy and a Kangaroo' by David R. Nicholas is from *Musical Wheat: Reflections on Life* (Blackburn: HarperCollins *Religious*, 1997), pp. 1–2.

'The Day God Burst Out of His Box' by Geoff Bullock is adapted from *Hands of Grace* (Sydney: Strand Publishing, 1998), pp. 82–6.

'The Great Maladikarra' by Dave Andrews is from *Christi-Anarchy* (Oxford: Lion Publishing, 1999), p. 101.

'All Before Lunch', © 2001 Sue Duggan.

'How Do We Choose Our Heroes?' by Mal Garvin is from *Breakthru* (Hornsby, NSW: Whitestone Books/Fusion, 1991) pp. 106–8.

'The Day the Creek Broke Its Banks', © 2001 Kel Richards. All fourteen of Kel Richards' *Bush Ballads* are available on CD from your local bookshop or direct from the publisher on (02) 9427 4197 or beacon@planet.net.au

'The Religious Fifth Column' by Fred Nile is condensed from *Fred Nile: An Autobiography* (Sydney: Strand Publishing, 2001), pp. 60–6.

'Hiding God's Word in My Heart', © 2001 Barry Chant.

'Missionaries Use Their Feet' by Phillip Jensen is adapted from *Southern Cross*, June 2001.

'The Fear of God' by Michael Frost is from *Jesus the Fool* (Sutherland, NSW: Albatross Books, 1994), pp. 17–18.

'According to His Purpose', © 2001 Gordon Moyes.

'Lessons from the Street' by Tim Costello is from *Streets of Hope* (Sydney: Allen & Unwin/Albatross Books, 1998), pp. 91–3.

'Baggage Boy' by Pat Mesiti is from *Dreamers Never Sleep* (Sydney: Self-published, 1996), pp. 58–9.

'What Would Jesus Do?' by Tracey Stewart is from *Payne Stewart: The Authorized Biography* (London: HarperCollins *Publishers*, 2000), pp. 263–4.

'Cop This!' by Grenville Kent is from *Signs of the Times*, June 2001, pp. 62–3.

'Penguins on Parade' by Philip Yancey is adapted from *Christianity Today*, © 1997 by Christianity Today International/Christianity Today Magazine. April 7, 1997, vol. 41, no 4, p. 72.

'Michael's Long Search', © 2001 Philip Johnson. Michael Graham's full story, *The Experience of Ultimate Truth*, will soon be published (for details see www.u-turnpress.com).

'The Day I Met the Wall With Hair' by Pat Mesiti is from *Dreamers Never Sleep* (Sydney: Self-published, 1996), pp. 6–10.

'Kill the Dill with the Pill' by Michael Frost is adapted from *Jesus the Fool* (Sutherland, NSW: Albatross Books, 1994), pp. 12–15.

'The Power of a Simple Invitation' by Margaret Reeson is from *No Fixed Address* (Sutherland, NSW: Albatross Books, 1991), pp. 18–21.

'The Kite Story', © 2001 Gillian Dixon.

'Praying in the Spirit' by Michael Frost is from *Eyes Wide Open* (Sutherland, NSW: Albatross Books, 1998), pp. 146–7.

'The "Twenty-Third" Bush Ballad', © 2001 Kel Richards. All fourteen
of Kel Richards' *Bush Ballards* are available on CD from your local
bookshop or direct from the publisher on (02) 9427 4197 or
beacon@planet.net.au

'Dean' by Dave Andrews is from *Christi-Anarchy* (Oxford: Lion
Publishing, 1999), pp. 105–6.

'Taking Up the Cross—21st Century Style', © 2001 Barry Chant.

'The Coober Pedy Cup' by Kerry Medway is from *Bush Preacher Bites
the Dust* (Sutherland, NSW: Albatross Books, 1983/Aussies Afire
Publishing, 1990, 1994), pp. 11–15.

'The Crazy Hitchhiker's Guide to Reality', © 2001 Ruth Pollard.

'Part of the Answer' by Gordon Moyes is adapted from *When Box Hill
Was a Village* (Anzea Books, 1991), pp. 129–36.

'The Childbirth Conspiracy' by Angela Eynaud is from *Alive Magazine*,
July 1999, p. 17.

'The Problem of Pain' by Phillip Jensen is adapted from *Southern Cross*,
Nov. 1999

'The Call of God' by Fred Nile is from *Fred Nile: An Autobiography*
(Sydney: Strand Publishing, 2001), pp. 53–4.

'The Platypus' by Ross Clifford and Philip Johnson is from *Riding the
Rollercoaster* (Sydney: Strand Publishing, 1998), pp. 37–8.

'The Ironman' by Michael Frost is adapted from *Longing for Love*
(Sutherland, NSW: Albatross Books), 1996, pp. 158–9.

'Love Spelled Y–O–U', © 2001 Glenn Williams. Glenn is the founder
and CEO of Focus on the Family Australia, an organisation

dedicated to strengthening Australia's families. For more information please visit their website (www.fofa.com.au).

'Shopping for Jeans' by Chad Armstrong is adapted from *Outreach*, June/July 2000, p. 16.

'Night Lights', © 2001 Kel Richards. All fourteen of Kel Richards' *Bush Ballads* are available on CD from your local bookshop or direct from the publisher on (02) 9427 4197 or beacon@planet.net.au

'The Big Picture of Ken Duncan' by Irene Voysey is adapted from *Signs of the Times*, June 1999, pp. 31–5.

'An Australian Elijah' by John Blacket is from *Fire in the Outback* (Sutherland: Albatross Books, 1997), pp. 63–4.

'A Day at the MCG' by Michael Frost is from *Eyes Wide Open* (Sutherland, NSW: Albatross Books, 1998), pp. 28–30.

'The King of Mintabi' by Kerry Medway is from *Bush Preacher Bites the Dust* (Sutherland, NSW: Albatross Books, 1983/Aussies Afire Publishing, 1990, 1994), pp. 100–7.

'Basketball Games' by Tim Costello is from *Tips from a Travelling Soul-Searcher* (Sydney: Allen & Unwin, 1999), pp. 85–6.

'Ankle Bob', © 2001 David R. Nicholas.

'My Version of Ecclesiastes 3:1–8' by Amanda Smith is from *Christian Woman*, May/June 2001.

'Cat Bites Man' by David R. Nicholas is from *Musical Wheat: Reflections on Life* (Blackburn: HarperCollins *Religious*, 1997), pp. 50–2.

'Jack Goldsmith—Outback Legend' by Nathan Brown is from *Signs of the Times*, March 2001, pp. 25–8.

'The Shared Meal' by Tim Costello is adapted from *Tips from a Travelling Soul-Searcher* (Sydney: Allen & Unwin, 1999), pp. 314–15, 318–19.

'God's Marbles' by Ken Duncan is adapted from *Spirit of Australia* (Ken Duncan Panographs, 1992) and *The Great Southland* (Ken Duncan Panographs, 1997).

'The Tale of Stumpy and Slick' by Barry Chant is from *Creative Living: How to Live the Kind of Life You've Always Wanted to Live* (South Plympton: Tabor Publications, 1996), pp. 143–7.

'The Whales' by Michael Frost is from *Eyes Wide Open* (Sutherland, NSW: Albatross Books, 1998), pp. 74–5.

'Off the Back of a Truck' by Margaret Reeson is from *No Fixed Address* (Sutherland, NSW: Albatross Books, 1991), pp. 235–6.

'Carols by Candlelight' by Mal Garvin, © 1998 Awakening 2000. Adapted.

'Better than Gold', © 2001 Gordon Moyes.

'The Rich Treasure of Forgiveness', © 2001 Kel Richards, from a forthcoming book, *Survivor*.